# THE BUDDHA'S CALL TO AWAKEN

*Shin Buddhist Views on the Crumbling of True Spiritual Values*

Monshu Koshin Ohtani

# THE BUDDHA'S CALL TO AWAKEN

*Shin Buddhist Views on the Crumbling of True Spiritual Values*

MONSHU KOSHIN OHTANI

AMERICAN BUDDHIST STUDY CENTER PRESS

NEW YORK

*The Buddha's Call to Awaken:*
*Shin Buddhist Views on the Crumbling of True Spiritual Values*

First edition 2012


English translation by W. S. Yokoyama
Based on the Japanese title, *Gu no chikara,*
Tokyo: Bungei Shunju, 2009

Edited and published by
American Buddhist Study Center Press, New York, NY
in collaboration with Buddhist Study Center, Honolulu, HI and
Buddhist Education Center, Anaheim, CA

Printed on 10% recycled paper with soy inks
Printed in the United States of America
Cover photo by Scott Mitchell
Design by Arlene Kato

Library of Congress Cataloging-in-Publication Data
Ohtani, Monshu Koshin,
*The Buddha's Call to Awaken:*
*Shin Buddhist Views on the Crumbling of True Spiritual Values*

ISBN 978-0-9764594-4-6



"Monshu" is the title of the head of the Nishi Hongwanji. Literally it means "Master of the Gate." The present Monshu is a direct descendant of Shinran Shonin, the founder of Shin Buddhism. In Japanese, an honorific prefix "Go" is added to the word "Monshu" which shows respect. Therefore, you will sometimes see the Monshu referred to as "Gomonshu," but the actual word and title is simply "Monshu."

# Contents

*Preface by Monshu Koshin Ohtani* *ix*

*Introduction by Alfred Bloom* *xi*

## THE BUDDHA'S CALL TO AWAKEN

*Shin Buddhist Views on the Crumbling of True Spiritual Values*

OPENING REMARKS 1

RESCRIPT 5

CHAPTER ONE
Living in an Age of Uncertainty 9

CHAPTER TWO
I Receive, Therefore I Am 25

CHAPTER THREE
Man is Bound to Die 49

CHAPTER FOUR
Shinran Shonin's Way of Life 79

CHAPTER FIVE
As Imperfect as We Are 101

CHAPTER SIX
Returning to the Foolish Nature of Our Self 133

BIBLIOGRAPHY 147

ACKNOWLEDGMENT 149

# PREFACE

On this occasion I am most pleased to announce the publication of my new book, *The Buddha's Call to Awaken*, from the American Buddhist Study Center, translated by W. Yokoyama. The original Japanese title, *Gu no chikara*, does not deal directly with the teachings of Jodo Shinshu, but, rather, discusses problematic points in Japanese society and life based on the teachings. We often think the world is becoming gradually better and more convenient as the economy develops and science and technology progress. Thinking how clever we are, though, gets the better of us when we forget all about our foolish side and actual limitations as human beings. Thus, when something terrible happens, the tragedy we experience is amplified on a scale we have never before encountered. Through these English translations it is my hope the Wisdom of the Buddhist teachings will find its place in the hearts of people everywhere.

Monshu Koshin Ohtani
Kyoto, Spring 2012

# Introduction

Monshu Ohtani Koshin assumed the office of Monshu in 1980. From the beginning of his tenure, he has striven to awaken the social awareness of the Nishi Hongwanji denomination of Shin Buddhism. He describes the ideal for members of the denomination: "Again, because he is awakened to the realization that the great Compassion of the Tathagata embraces all men equally and constantly, his is a life of brotherhood and mutual trust in all men. Therefore, he is able to break out from the shell of isolation, egocentricity, and selfishness and become actively concerned with society and its well-being. This also, at once, should be the response of the total Hongwanji organization that will have an open door to the world."

He came into office as Japan confronted ecological, economic and social changes that have raised questions about the meaning of life and the relevance of religion in modern society. He has deeply observed how the world's economic expansion, as well as technological advances, have threatened the meaning of life, while also increasing our material benefits. Therefore at the conclusion of his first *Rescript* given four years into his tenure, he noted that the value of a religion is determined by its response to such conditions that bring anxiety and suffering to mankind, declaring: "Fully aware of the heritage from the Founder Shinran Shonin, I am determined not to rest within the comparative quiet of a closed door, but as a Nembutsu devotee of this new era I will take a meaningful and positive step to strengthen and enlarge the circle of Nembutsu and advance the good and welfare of all people."

The progress of modern life has stimulated greed which seeks wealth beyond personal needs and the acquisition of personal goods in excess. As the Monshu notes, animals only consume what they need, while humans seek much more than they require. The problem is more than making money or accumulating things. It is not simply that material prosperity crushes the human spirit. Rather, without a decline in the human spirit, material prosperity cannot prevail. "It is at the cost of the human spirit that material prosperity exists." The loss of the human spirit began before the rise in material prosperity and made it possible.

Monshu Ohtani views our contemporary problems as a spiritual problem which results from a "human-centered way of thinking" by which he means making "Humanity as an absolute standard." This view assumes everything should revolve around a human-being's point of view. It has been a great force leading to the progress of science and technology and the resultant crumbling of true spiritual values which has brought on the flux of material prosperity.

To be human-centered means to place everything under the dominance and control of humans. Such dominance, however, is contrary to Buddhism whose perspective embraces the whole realm of sentient beings. "It is not just human beings, but all living things, all that have the breath of life, that are the object of liberation in Buddhism." This means that any approach to the resolution of modern problems must have a holistic perspective, taking account of its implications for all living beings and the environment.

Though lamenting modern human-centered thinking, Monshu Ohtani employed the phrase "our sense of being human," as a means of communicating spiritual values to modern people. He emphasizes "what one might call the religious in our life, the sense of our going beyond this world to a dimension of spirituality that lies beyond."

Next, he pointed out that he also used the phrase to urge people to awaken unto themselves, to return to the point where they enter into dialogue with themselves. He states that, "It is not until we have an awakening unto ourselves, and by this I mean an acknowledgment of our irrepressible blind desires, an awakening to our sense of being evil and unwell, an awakening to our limitations, that we can begin 'to restore our true sense of being human' and at last learn to live in earnest. It was in order to evoke this self-awakening in people that I chose the wording in question."

However, the use of this phrase raised questions within the Shin community. The Monshu understands this problem because Shin Buddhism views human nature as corrupt, and, therefore, being human in the modern sense is ambiguous. His project, however, is to call people back to the spiritual foundation of life as viewed by Shinran. Contrary to Shinran, modern humanism views human nature as essentially good, while obstacles to the achievement of that good must be cleared away. Further, people generally believe that it is through their own ingenuity and science that they can solve problems themselves. Therefore, to advance his message, Monshu Ohtani critiques the widely understood, modern view, while humbly suggesting the alternative found in Shinran's thought.

Shinran's understanding of human nature, based in Buddhism and his own experience, highlights the term *Gu*, foolishness, ignorance or unawareness. It is essential in modern society to understand this term, describing the reality of our individual lives, in order to limit the damage done by human greed through the exploitation of people and the domination of nature in modern societies. By recognizing Shinran's understanding of foolishness (Gu) within ourselves, the true equality of people can emerge and our many problems can be mitigated by understanding our mutual limitations and our interdependence with others. The title of the Japanese edition: *The Power of Foolishness* (*Gu no chikara*) gains its significance from the new vision of society that it implies. We can only fulfill our human ideals when we recognize the power of foolishness in our lives. The recognition of foolishness makes clear the true nature of human beings and clarifies our responsibility to nature and society.

To appreciate the Monshu's stress on Shinran's understanding of Gu/Foolishness/Ignorance and blind passion we should note here that Shinran did not originate the principle of Gu. It has been a long-standing principle from the beginning of Buddhism that sentient beings are foolish beings enmeshed in fundamental ignorance of their true nature, and thereby arousing blind passions and evil acts. Over the history of Buddhism, it was assumed that with the removal of ignorance and passion, enlightenment would ensue.

In Pure Land Buddhism this came to be termed the Saintly Path, the path of rigorous discipline and difficult practices, pursued in a monastery. Teachers in the Pure Land tradition also understood that without the assistance (Other Power) of Amida Buddha, given in his name, ordinary people would have dim hope of attaining enlightenment and emancipation from the stream of births and deaths. Therefore, as part of their practice they advocated the meritorious recitation of Amida's name as the means established by the Buddha's vow, for ordinary people to gain birth in the Pure Land where conditions would be available to assure enlightenment.

Shinran, however, as a result of his own spiritual failure in practice on Mount Hiei and his life-changing study with Honen, came to the conclusion that the depth of ignorance and blind passion made it impossible for any person, no matter how spiritually proficient, to gain enlightenment without the compassion of Amida Buddha. The fundamental ignorance and blind passions remain even in exalted practice. For Shinran, it is through awakening to our true nature as deeply ignorant, passion-ridden foolish beings in a personal and existential way that opens the door to our enlightenment and the world of equality and mutual human responsibilities that can solve or mitigate our problems.

Shin Buddhism is a teaching of transformation whereby broken shards are transformed to gold. Monshu Ohtani, through his work, interprets many significant aspects of Shinran's thought, highlighting Shinran's distinctive contribution not only for the religious world, but also in society.

What is most significant about this volume is that Monshu Ohtani wrote it in the context of the various problems and crises that have beset humanity in Japan and the world during his tenure. He looks beyond the simply personal nature of religion and its otherworldly character to see the Buddha calling modern people to take the teaching seriously and grasp their responsibility to care for the world and society. He calls us to return to our awareness of our deep ignorance and foolishness, to return to our true nature in order to resolve the crises. It is important that the Monshu not merely calls for personal piety, but challenges us to become more aware of our global society and how our faith can relate to it constructively and positively. His writing in this volume and other texts consistently urges Shin Buddhists to work for a better world, creating a world of *Annon Nare*, a peaceful world.

Alfred Bloom
Professor Emeritus
University of Hawai'i

# The Buddha's Call to Awaken

*Shin Buddhist Views on the Crumbling of True Spiritual Values*

# Opening Remarks

At present we stand at a great turning point in history. As we assume our role therein, ours is an age of uncertainty, burdened as it is with numerous problems in our lives as individuals as well as members of society.

As the bonds of society erode, people have become increasingly isolated from one another. With the advent of a time when people can expect to live into their eighties, this ushers in an age of hope for them as well as a good deal of trepidation regarding the life process of birth, aging, sickness, and death.

The economic crisis that befell the world in the autumn of 2008 has only increased the feelings of uncertainty that now beset us daily.

There are people who suddenly find themselves dismissed and out of a job. There are young people who are shut out of companies they wished to apply to. There are housewives who must now look for part-time work. There are seniors who wonder how they can make ends meet on their meager retirement pensions.

This once-in-a-century economic crisis took experts by surprise and led them to make conflicting analyses of the situation.

None of their conclusions are entirely mistaken, of course.

The root source of the present crisis lies in a problem that I identified some thirty years ago when I was appointed Monshu to the Jodo Shinshu Hongwanji-ha. That is the problem of "human-centered thinking."

This huge crisis that we are confronting, that threatens to engulf the world and is causing us endless worry, is not merely an economic problem. People are beginning to realize that it has come about because we are reaching the limits of our "human-centered" approach to life.

Mahatma Gandhi believed that it is a sign of an unhealthy society when people live in a world where they engage in economic activity that must always reap a profit. This is exactly what our society has become.

And what lies in the background of this model of society is the thinking that we as errant human beings should run the world and control every aspect of it.

It is not mere coincidence that this world economic crisis should have begun in America. America is the country that has promoted the idea that human beings should be in control of everything.

There is no limit to human greed. Animals that have voracious appetites will eat their fill and then eat no more. Humans, by contrast, will eat their fill and still continue to gorge themselves to the point of illness.

It is the same with money. It is said that some CEOs of investment banks in America made profits of several billions or tens of billions of dollars. People want to make a great deal of money for which they have no possible use. This is what caused the economic disaster on a worldwide scale.

One would think that living a long life of eighty years would be enough, but that is not the case. People want to live an even longer and healthier life.

Buddhism has long concerned itself with the problem of insatiable desires. Only an awakened person, that is, a Buddha, can truly overcome these desires. While such a feat might fall within the capability of a person of spiritual excellence, it proves an insurmountable problem for ordinary people like ourselves.

As we look back on history, we can see no solution to the problem of human desires. Though it goes without saying that a person and his desires go hand in hand, one cannot be allowed to indulge them unchecked; hence, the problem of human desire has long been a problem addressed by religion.

In the Jodo Shinshu founder Shinran Shonin's *Kyogyoshinsho*, we come across a critical statement that he left us on his own life when he said, "I am someone who is constantly drowning in the vast sea of love and desire." Such "love and desire" is not a reference simply to the love and desire between a man and a woman. It points, rather, to the broader meaning of "human beings" drowning in the ocean of lust and desires. Jodo Shinshu teaches that if it was within human capacity to have complete control of our love and desire, then there would be no need for us to be saved by Amida Buddha. It is because we have only limited control that we turn to Amida for liberation.

Shinran Shonin would also admit that he was only human, that he was just another ordinary being afflicted with irresistible blind desires. Shinran Shonin's teacher, Honen Shonin (founder of Jodoshu), would advise us of the importance of acknowledging our "foolish nature."

It is because we are these foolish beings that we need liberation by Amida Buddha. This is important to remember about the Pure Land teaching.

Shinran Shonin lived in a turbulent time. Indeed, Shinran had to strive mightily to live through this period of turmoil in order to introduce the great changes he did to the Buddhist world.

In Japan's aging society, where the family structure is under threat and people are growing increasingly estranged from one another, the situation has deteriorated to the point that anyone who is not a friend is to be regarded with suspicion. When ethical standards were in decline and the feeling of uncertainty arose, worldwide economic crisis struck.

As each of us strives to live through this period of change, we find ourselves mired in the problems begotten by "human-centered" thinking that stare us in the face.

On the occasion of Shinran Shonin's 750$^{th}$ Memorial Service in 2011, we offer this book introducing the life and thought of Shinran Shonin. With the concepts of "ordinary beings" and "foolish beings" taught by Honen Shonin and Shinran Shonin as a guide, it would be of benefit if we could all work together to change this way of life that is skewed by this "human-centered" way of thinking.

# Rescript

*On the Occasion of*
*The Accession Commemorative Celebrations*
*April 1, 1980*

## Religion in the Contemporary World

The ultimate solution for the sufferings of illness, old-age, and death lies in religion. The Renunciation of Sakyamuni Buddha was motivated by his realization of these sufferings, and mankind cannot but seek the meaning of life when confronted by approaching illness, old-age, and death. Herein lies the fundamental significance of religion which seeks liberation from suffering.

Man lives within the confines of history, and society and religion, too, cannot survive if they deny this fact. The present is an age of unprecedented cycles of changes brought about by the rapid developments in science, technology, and industry, and these fluxions deeply affect the minds of mankind.

The advances of technology and economics have made the realization of man's dreams possible, but at the same time they have increased his greed and avarice beyond bounds. This egocentric desire disregards others and gives birth to inequality and discrimination. The isms that emphasized man of course brought about his liberation and equality, but these also caused him to become an absolute unto himself and begot strife and insecurity.

The swift urbanization of society causes the weakening of the sense of community solidarity and the growing centralized control results in eroding the foundation upon which the individual can rely causing him to forfeit himself and in the end depriving him of his capacity to correctly see others, their personalities, and even the nobility of life itself. Moreover, these factors highly influence the development of civilization and culture as well as religion by undermining the standards of their traditions.

In this critical period when man's very existence becomes questionable, religion must not be just a temporary diversion.

Today's religion has the responsibility of teaching the way by which mankind can truly become humanized. It behooves us, the religionists, not to ingratiate ourselves to secular powers, but to become fully knowledgeable of the teaching in which we place our faith and courageously walk the path to Truth hand in hand with those of the same faith. Furthermore, we must not forget to hold earnest dialogues with others whose religions are historically and traditionally rich in truth.

## Jodo Shinshu and the Responsibility of Its Devotees

The nembutsu doctrine of Jodo Shinshu founded by Shinran Shonin has been handed down to us these more than 700 years by the succeeding generations of our faithful forebears. The teaching is rich in tradition, but there is a tendency today to drift into formalism. It is, therefore, necessary for us to deeply reflect and rediscover within that tradition the true spirit of the Founding Father.

Jodo Shinshu teaches us that we are blessed with faith through the work of the Primal Vow-power, and by living in the nembutsu we shall be given the beneficence of birth and buddhahood in the Pure Land. He who hears and has faith in this Dharma and lives resolutely with the nembutsu is the true devotee. He places absolute reliance in the Primal Vow of Amida Buddha and fully aware that he is a simpleton, subject to birth and death and filled with avarice, anger, and malcontent, leads a life of contrition.

Again, because he is awakened to the realization that the great Compassion of the Tathagata embraces all men equally and constantly, his is a life of brotherhood and mutual trust in all men. Therefore, he is able to break out from the shell of isolation, egocentricity, and selfishness and become actively concerned with society and its well-being. This also, at once, should be the response of the total Hongwanji organization that will have an open door to the world.

This open door policy underlines the main program of our Hongwanji and shall see its positive manifestation in the people to people relationships that will be developed. Of course the propagation of faith in the nembutsu will be pursued so that each of us can become a true devotee, but the responsibility for the well-being of the world-at-large today and tomorrow shall be shouldered as our own. It is vital, then, that we endeavor to firmly establish within ourselves the doctrinal foundation and, extending beyond the confines of the Hongwanji, propagate the teaching widely throughout the world, and looking to the future educate and enrich the lives of youth of today with religious culture. Herein lies the materialization of the true development of the Hongwanji.

In the face of the many complex problems that bring anxiety and suffering to mankind the worth of a true religion is discovered. Fully aware of the heritage from the Founder Shinran Shonin, I am determined not to rest within the comparative quiet of a closed door, but as a nembutsu devotee of this new era I will take a meaningful and positive step to strengthen and enlarge the circle of nembutsu and advance the good and welfare of all people.

Chapter 1

# Living in an Age of Uncertainty

*The ocean of birth-and-death,*
*of painful existence, has no bound.*
—*Koso wasan*

## Humanity's Life or Death Crisis

I was thirty-one when I became the Monshu of our Hongwanji. I was relatively young when I took up the post, compared to the *kanshus* (head priests) and *kanchos* (abbots) of the other Buddhist denominations. In order to let the ministers and sangha members of our tradition know what was on my mind, I published the *Rescript*. That was in 1980, in the fourth year of my role as Monshu.

At that time I used the phrase, "Humanity's life or death crisis." I would have to admit that the statement, "Humanity's life or death crisis," might have been a bit overblown, but what was on my mind as I set it down was the strong conviction that our age had reached a critical turning point.

This period, from the 1970s to the 1980s, achieved a high degree of economic growth, and scientific advances and economic development were such that countless numbers of humanity's fondest dreams came true. How the sparkle of that time seemed to promise an even brighter future!

However, while some dreams were realized, this period also witnessed an unbridled expansion of greed as we plunged ever deeper into the abyss of self-centeredness where the only thing that mattered was feeding our own personal craving for more. It was during this time that I assumed office; however, I was definitely of a mind not to rest content to watch the age proceed along in this manner.

In 1962, Rachel Carson published her famous book *Silent Spring*, which brought the problem of pollution to public awareness. In 1972, the Club of Rome published *The Limits to Growth*, and in the eighties we started to realize that the problem went beyond simply blaming industry for causing pollution, and that this was in fact a problem taking place on a worldwide scale.

Indeed, this was an age when we clearly realized the responsibility that we bore for pursuing a "human-centered" way of thinking.

## Humanity's Spirit Has to be Broken For Material Prosperity to Prevail

In 1973, our Jodo Shinshu Hongwanji-ha denomination celebrated the anniversary of Shinran Shonin's 800$^{th}$ year and the establishment of his teaching's 750$^{th}$ year with a great *Hoyo* Dharma service and various events. For me this corresponded with my final year as a graduate student, and a subtle shift is evident in what I think now and what I thought then.

Around that time I was quite fond of the phrase "material prosperity leads to the crushing of the human spirit" and would often use it in sermons. What I would say in effect was, "We should not give in to material prosperity; we should also strive to elevate ourselves spiritually and culturally, and to that end we should make it a rule to do without material things." However, it occurred to me that I had gotten everything turned around.

It is not a matter of "Material prosperity leads to the crushing of the human spirit," but rather, "Without the breaking of the human spirit, material prosperity cannot prevail." I would contend, and on this I would hope you agree, that it is more to the point to say that "It is at the cost of the human spirit that material prosperity exists."

## There Is a Limit to Our Natural Resources

At the beginning of the seventies, no one pondered these matters at great length. Our national slogan at the time was "To be in harmony with human progress." It was the general belief that, along with scientific progress, the problems of pollution and poverty, as well as religious issues, would no longer exist. And so believing, without ascertaining the situation, without stopping to think, without reflecting more deeply on the matter, Japan as a whole simply rushed off in a mad dash in that direction.

My use of the phrase "humanity's life or death crisis" indicates the reservations I had about believing naively in the kind of future that science and technology promised to carve out for us, as well as the sense of crisis I felt as to whether it was possible for us to live in harmony with such progress. It was also around this time that the novelist Ariyoshi Sawako's two-volume work *Fukugo Osen*, on the dangers of compound contaminants, was published.

There was also the oil shock. In 1973, when the price of crude oil skyrocketed, petroleum products and related goods, and even toilet paper, started to vanish from the store shelves, causing a great panic among consumers. The lesson the oil shock taught us was that natural resources are limited. It gave a country like Japan, which does not have such resources, an opportunity to pause for thought and contemplate what she would have to do in this situation.

However, once the worst had passed and life settled back to normal, people quickly put the crisis out of their minds. The fact that there is a limit to things, that is, the awareness of the limited nature of things, stopped at the level of turning to technology to come up with energy-saving means, and did not penetrate deep into our psyche. We will return to this topic later on, but this awareness of the limited nature of things is basic to the Buddhist way of thinking.

Once again we are faced with a crisis in natural resources and food supplies. Neither the Japanese nor the Americans have done a single thing to seriously consider the problem of their living in this "human-centered" way. In the case of Japan, from the mid-eighties to the nineties, and in America, during the twenty-first century, we have danced on a bubble economy, indulging our desires in earnest, until the bubble burst, yet even now there is not the slightest indication that we intend to change our ways.

## It is Ludicrous to Live in This "Human-centered" Way

In the same *Rescript*, I used the term "human-centered" thinking and "Humanity as an absolute standard." This was to point out that it is not just human beings, but all living things, all that have the breath of life, that are the object of liberation in Buddhism.

Opposing this is the view that everything should revolve around a human-being's point of view. This way of thinking has even been called the great force driving our age. I've said that the crumbling of true spiritual values is what brought on the flux of material prosperity, but it seems that even before that time, the

Buddhist world view, as well as the Buddhist view of human life, had been virtually lost.

At that juncture I used the words, "We must restore our true sense of being human." However, when the *Rescript* was published, those words were met with a flurry of doubts.

In the Jodo Shinshu tradition, from the very beginning a human being is regarded to be lost in blind desires enmeshed in irrepressible urges. When a person lost in blind desires receives the awakening of *shinjin* through Other Power; that is, not through his selfish power, he becomes a person of the nembutsu, and as a true disciple of the Buddha, he goes on to be born in the Pure Land where he perfects buddhahood. Thus the word "humanity" is not always given a positive meaning in Jodo Shinshu.

Why then did I use the words, "We must restore our true sense of being human?" Even if we call for an evolution of thought beyond the "human-centered" one, such an expression is too far removed from the language of everyday life. While it might have made sense among the ministers of the Hongwanji organization, it cannot be said to get through to the ordinary person, and would be ineffective to get them to resist the notion of humanity as the so-called great force driving the age. Out of consideration for those who are not familiar with Jodo Shinshu terminology, and in order to point people towards a goal that we all share, I made an exception to use the phrase "our sense of being human" or "humanity."

Though it is in the Pure Land that we become buddhas, in this world we must follow the ways of the world and live our lives with the goal of being true disciples of the Buddha.

It is, indeed, the case that the general usage of the phrase, "our sense of being human" or "humanity" apart from the Jodo Shinshu teaching tends to be vague and to invite misunderstanding. After all, a human being has various potentials, and his humanity includes the potential for good as well as the potential for evil. And so the question of what is true humanity is asked.

First, as to my reason for using "our sense of being human," I wished to point out that there is what one might call the religious in our life, the sense of our going beyond this world to a dimension of spirituality that lies beyond. In the case of Buddhism, this is to open up the dimension of spirituality by, or through enlightenment. Other religions also have this feature and that is what makes a religion. In our life in this world as individual human beings, then, rather than always being a slave to our self-centered desires, I had hoped that we would strive to go beyond that level to restore "our true sense of being human" even to a small degree.

Next, my other reason for using "our sense of being human" was to urge people to awaken unto themselves, to return to the point where they enter into dialogue with themselves. It is not until we have an awakening unto ourselves, and by this I mean an acknowledgment of our irrepressible blind desires, an awakening to our sense of being evil and unwell, an awakening to our limitations, that we can begin "to restore our true sense of being human" and at last learn to live in earnest. It was in order to evoke this self-awakening in people that I chose the wording in question.

Finally, my intention in using the words "to restore our true sense of being human" was to bring into relief the various critical scenarios that are being manifested when we errant human beings put ourselves at the center and make ourselves the absolute standard for all things.

## Seriously, Now, Do We Really Want to Live a Long Life?

Recently the media gave pollution problems major coverage, throwing a spotlight on the damage they inflicted. The discernible causes of the damage were of course duly investigated by the media; however, no one thought to inquire as to the ultimate source from which these problems arose. That is, no one thought to address the basic problem with regard to the economic policy of putting fiscal growth first; this aspect was never considered and examined.

In our contemporary time, people have held the view that, since science and technology had made this mess, the same science and technology should progress to the point where they would clean it up. This was the thinking behind Japan's national slogan, "To be in harmony with human progress." Such thinking extends even to the present day.

If science and technology would only come up with products that were even a little less damaging, the thinking is, that would help to reduce the problem with the products themselves. When we look at it from that narrow point of view, it would seem that, why, yes, indeed, we are making headway with the problem. However, while it is possible to say that these products are less damaging than before, does it really make sense to continue to expand the wholesale production and consumption of such products? Imagine what would happen if the whole world were to say, "I want to live a pleasant and comfortable life."

Even with regard to the sub-prime loans that triggered the economic collapse, there were experts who said that if only the financial world could have improved its methods, all of this would not have happened. Seen from the point of view of financial investors with limited resources to invest, if the risky mortgages were bundled together and sold as securities, and managed with a bit of oversight to turn a profit, wouldn't that be a grand idea? It did not seem to occur to these bankers that the risk involved put the livelihoods and futures of countless people at risk. Whatever it takes to turn a profit is one way to look at it, but seriously, now, is that really what we want?

There are scholars who predict that with the scientific advances and medical techniques of anti-aging, it will be possible for a person to live to be 120 years of age. However, even if all people were to live to be 120 years old, what kind of world would that be? Even now, our present so-called aging society is not always spoken of in glowing terms. Indeed, the more that our society advances in age, the greater our feelings of uncertainty, as the prevailing opinion is that these old people pose a burden to society. People say, "I want to live a long life," but one wonders whether happiness awaits.

When you sit quietly and contemplate this world and your life in it, however convenient, rich, or long a life you may live, first you have to gauge whether these things you long for will decrease your sense of uneasiness or increase it. Once you do that, I think you will find a way to put those feelings of uncertainty to work for you.

## Why This Uneasy Feeling?

Originally, the problem at hand was not one of scientific technology, but the problem of life or the problem of human existence.

Measured in terms of average life expectancy, monetary wealth, and material prosperity, the problem of life is that the modern world encompasses the sum total of who I am. This is itself the source of anxiety. Unless some significant change in values takes place on a larger scale with a great number of people, not just a few, there is no solution forthcoming.

Indeed, what many people are beginning to realize is that scientific and technological progress or material prosperity provide no solution to the problem. What grates, though, is that we can discover no other values to replace them. As a result there is no way to summarily dispel our sense of unease.

Oddly enough, we are experiencing this feeling of uncertainty in the midst of prosperity. Modern people are suffering in an age blessed with such wealth as would astound the imagination of anyone who has lived through hard times and had to scrape to get by.

When our spirits are broken, we become reduced to being put to work as tools of organizations or tools of industry. People are not only used and managed simply to provide labor: the very source of our being, the human spirit, is made into a tool. So it is that we cannot shake off this feeling of uncertainty that gnaws at us.

Around the eighties, when the Japanese work force was harnessed to rebuild the country and society, the laborers were called society's army of cogs. Today it is the consumer age. The government has even created a department of consumer affairs. It seems that our army of cogs has moved up in the world.

In our economic activities, we are both the producers and the consumers. As consumers, though, it is not always the necessities or basic foodstuffs that we buy. Often it is something we can do without that has no bearing on our survival, but clever advertising leads us to buy it by pitching it to us as something we cannot live without. Caught in this mad storm of mass production and mass consumption, we have become people who live only to fulfill our desires. This tendency grows ever stronger. It is where our "human-centered" way of life is taking us.

## Well, Everyone Else is Doing It...

What is the consumer like?

When we examine what the consumer is really like, we find that when a person is a consumer, it is because they are being managed as such. It is not industry that is managing them. The whole world is out to buy things that are impossible for people to afford. Whether it is a cell phone or computer game that Johnny wants, he pesters his parents by saying, "Well, everyone else has one." And it is not just the children; both the purchasing adults and the ones for whom they buy things are all the same.

"Everyone else is buying one." "Everyone else is doing it." "Everyone else is saying it."

With "everyone else" as a reason, everyone starts moving in the same direction without the least thought. It was the same with World War II, and it is the same with Japan's postwar plan for long term economic growth.

Whether it was Japan's sudden entry into war with America or the long term economic growth, we can sense the same pattern being repeated with the "power of the times" as the driving force. No one noticed the frightening "power of the times" that swept everyone away without allowing them a moment to stop and think.

It was also the same with our bubble economy. Everyone thought that stocks should rise and that land prices should go up, and that was what happened to the economy.

What can we say except, we get uneasy when we are not doing what everyone else is doing.

What can we say except, we get uneasy if we do not share the same sense of values as everyone else. That just goes to show how lonely and isolated our lives have become these days.

## Drowning in Our Success

It is too bad that economic growth was the only thing we could find in the postwar Japanese sense of values. As we entered the twenty-first century, we began to notice how difficult it was to maintain this trajectory of constant growth. Nothing has changed, however, with regard to our sense of values, and this is cause for a new sense of uncertainty. In extreme cases a social problem will occur when someone goes off the deep end and becomes hysterical and attacks someone, or conversely, becomes afraid of the outside world and falls into depression.

It is possible to try to step beyond the problem by harkening back to the good old days or turning to nationalism. The problem, however, remains. Unless we can address the root source of the problem, that is, the hollowing out of the Japanese spirit, we can talk all we want about how times were better before or how we should take a strong stance for nationalism, but this leads nowhere. The policy of placing fiscal growth first has only been replaced by nationalism.

Technological progress and economic development have made our material dreams come true, one after another, and their very success has made us lose sight of one very important matter. It could be that this lapse on the part of the Japanese is an especially strong tendency in postwar Japan. Though we are drowning in this success story that has been called the miracle of Asia, Japan is smugly satisfied that we Japanese are the only ones swimming in the material prosperity we have achieved. Even after this success story had its bubble burst with the collapse of the bubble economy, the smug attitude of the Japanese, that as long as it is good for us Japanese alone that is all that matters, has not changed in the least.

A while ago, this was noted by the Hongwanji Press publication titled, *Our Economy Has Seen Growth, But Has Our Spirit?* Although our economy has grown, it accounts for only a small part of the entire world economy. Even if we look at Japan alone, there are still many sick and poor people who are suffering, so many that saying "our economy has grown and we are better off" seems to be out of touch with reality. This would have to mean that we are not counting the homeless among us as one of "us." I once had to tell a member of our *kyodan* (sangha) that, if that is what you mean, I would hope one should think twice before making that kind of statement.

It is one thing when you speak as an individual, but when you speak in the collective "we," we cannot turn a blind eye to the suffering of the poor, or that will mean we are putting the suffering of the people who are starving completely out of our minds.

As individuals it is very much the case that we are living in the lap of luxury. When I compare our country today to the Japan of my youth, we are now astonishingly well off. The other day I was surprised to hear my daughter say that there are no schools in Japan that do not have air conditioning. I surprised her in turn when I told her that I do not recall ever having studied in an air-conditioned classroom.

Our present wealth and success have been established in a narrow gauge, and we only see what we want to see. If it spoils our satisfaction with our success, we simply ignore it. This narrowness of outlook is seen all across society. When this so-called wealth is brought to face the marked poverty of the rest of the world, it simply turns its back to it, as if it had seen nothing at all. Unless we see that this lopsided wealth is the cause of the uneasiness in society and the world, we are bound to repeat the same situation that led to the subprime loans.

## We Must Not Give in to This Feeling of Uncertainty

The words "*Okagesama*" and "*arigato*," meaning "thanks to you" and "thank you," were chosen by my father, the previous Monshu, as a theme for the 800th Anniversary of Shinran Shonin's birth in 1973.

The tenure of the former Monshu, that is, the period when my father was the Monshu, encompassed the time from before the start of World War II, to that of the Sino-Japanese War of 1937 to 1945, and culminated in the Pacific War that ended in Japan's defeat. After her defeat, the country started from zero and the economy revived. In 1973, people still believed that the world economy would continue to improve.

If the present era is an age of uncertainty, that time was an era of optimism.

This well expresses the feeling of the time and the good reputation it had, and the words were heard spoken by just about everyone. It was remarkable how easily the words "thanks for everything" and "thank you" slipped into our way of life so as to virtually become a physical part of it. However, at that time the awareness of our having reached a great turning point in history had yet to emerge.

As I wrote in my *Rescript,* "When a person is awakened to realize that he is a foolish being of karmic evil caught in birth and death, the life that he leads is one of joy and gratitude." This is not as easily understood as the previous Monshu's "thanks for everything" and "thank you." Nor does it exactly spill forth effortlessly from our lips.

What does it mean to awaken to the fact that we are just ordinary beings?

To be a *bombu*, or "just another ordinary being," is an important term in the teaching of Shinran Shonin; however, it is difficult to capture the kind of life style that the concept implies.

At a Zen temple the bulletin board will have a motto posted, saying, "A man of few wants knows satisfaction." That, in a nutshell, is the Zen life style—how extremely easy it is to understand!

Even in the Pure Land Buddhist teachings' admonitions to "awaken to acknowledging one's foolish being and ignorant self," are not simple and clear-cut. Even our relatively familiar terms such as *jiriki* and *tariki*, meaning "self-power" and "power beyond self," as well as *akunin*, meaning "evil person," easily lend themselves to misunderstanding. However, from the very start, our daily lives are far from being simple and clear-cut, and it is hardly ever that we can arrive at a swift solution to our problems.

The danger I sense with recent spiritual healing movements is that they do not allow us to think matters out for ourselves, and instead offer clear-cut solutions for problems that we have that are far from clear-cut. They will tell you that your problems are being caused by a bad spirit that has latched onto you. They conjure up this spirit on which they place all the blame. Or else they tell you of a way to save yourself by a miracle cure. Those who are looking for quick answers will leap at the opportunity.

When such faith movements enjoy a huge surge of popularity, it means that traditional religions, my own included, are not answering to the needs of people living in this age of anxiety. Indeed, people are putting themselves at risk by relying on easy solutions.

To live in this age of uncertainty, though we are ill at ease it is no simple matter to rid ourselves of this feeling of uncertainty, and so it is important that we learn to not give in to it. I think we can say that the orientation of the Pure Land Buddhist teachings urge us to be just another ordinary person and to awaken to our foolish self. This is one helpful point we can learn.

In the next chapter we will inquire into the cause of the difficulty in living in the present age, delving into the meaning of the phrase "all living beings."

## Chapter 2

# I Receive, Therefore I Am

*For all sentient beings, without exception, have been our parents and brothers and sisters in the course of countless lives in many states of existence.*
*—A Record in Lament of Divergences*

## The Little Importance Attached to Life

Although the so-called human-centered way of thinking claims to put people at the center, the result is that little importance is attached to the life of each person. We are reminded of this disregard for life every time we hear a news report of some crime. It is not always the case that the number of murder cases will rise constantly; if we look only at vicious crimes, there might even be a reduction. Of the cases that are hard to understand, though, there is the criminal who does not want to die alone and so finds an innocent bystander whose life he takes, fully expecting to be sentenced to death for his crime. This shows that people are attaching too little importance to their own lives as well as the lives of others.

Why has the world come to this?

Right now, in society today, we do not have a feeling of life, of being alive in relation to others — this is the problem.

Throughout history, the love of one's parents is most important; this is a constant. We are the object of our parents' affections, we are trusted by them, and whatever we do is applauded by them. It is this feedback from the key people in our lives, this real feeling of being loved by them, that is missing.

This is not just between parent and child. Our lives have many layers and in the course of the day we will have dealings with many people; our grandparents, our relatives, our neighbors, our school friends, our teachers, our co-workers, and even our parents' friends. And yet the feedback that tells us that we are living, the vivid sense we are alive, is just not there.

This has nothing to do with whether or not we are managing our lives wisely; it goes beyond such considerations. What it comes down to is the way we are being responded to as a people, as human beings —this contributes immensely to our will to live. When a person no longer shares a place where he feels these bonds of kinship, a place where he can laugh with others and cry with others, he is no longer able to live.

In the vicinity of the Hongwanji in Kyoto, where I make my home, we have what is called a neighborhood association. This association makes sure everyone in the community knows who their neighbors are. When they meet they greet each other with the usual pleasantries and they even go to the assistance of neighbors who are in need. I would venture to say that young people today have lost this sense of place. Living in an apartment in a mass housing project in a big city, or buying a house in a tract in the suburbs, you are just there, completely unrelated to anyone else. It could well be that such a person does not even have a sense of being isolated.

## The Struggle to Find Yourself

There was a time when the phrase "finding yourself" was popular. In the present age where people feel isolated and they do not have that feedback from life that connects them with their immediate world, it becomes necessary for one to "find oneself." It may be the present society's demand for individuality that drives this need to "find oneself."

In the previous chapter, we talked about how "everyone else is doing it," where, like it or not, we are under social pressure to conform. On the other hand, at home and at school it is demanded that we each show our unique individuality and children are brought up with an emphasis on drawing out their own special talent.

In life, if someone does something that makes them stand out, their parents will take them aside and caution them that it is better to keep a low profile if you don't want people to get on your case. At the same time, the parents will sing the same litany about how much better it is to educate our children to respect individuality and how each child should have their own unique personality. This is a major contradiction.

This contradiction, which is forced on young people, is unbearable. As a result, their lives become a race for individuality. When everyone around you becomes your rival it is impossible to form strong friendships.

From the time we were young, we had the real feeling of being loved by our parents, and being praised by those around us. As we grew older it was also important for us to feel useful. These experiences affirming our existence are essential to our real sense of living.

In the past, children used to help out at home and go out on errands, but I do not recall hearing such talk these days. There was a time when the Boy Scouts and Girl Scouts, who perform important community services, were much more active. It might not be easy for one person to do much, but when you do it as part of a group like the scouts, it is possible to make some headway.

Nor do I notice children playing baseball in the park as much. Even the children on the playground are fewer in number. Places where we can meet our friends, where we can laugh together and cry together, have disappeared. There are also fewer adults who are able to provide that kind of environment for children. The adults are having a hard time making ends meet, especially if they have been laid off or their companies have gone out of business.

Young people are absorbed in their cell phones, personal computers, and computer games. At a glance these devices would seem to connect them with each other, but the truth is these young people are not connected to anyone at all. With no real connection, their sense of isolation only increases. I see this in the swagger of those who are arrested for violent crimes.

Although children are raised to become individuals and diverse, and even though adults expect this of them — or rather, because it is expected of them—they instead conform to a smug, self-righteous way of life. This plunges these children ever deeper into isolation.

This is the flip side of affluence, living the good life. I have my own room, I don't have to go out; I can just shut the door and live like this. This kind of life is only possible in a society that is materially well-off. After all there are any number of societies where children have to work to live or are forced to enlist as soldiers.

On the surface it would seem that our society with its falling birthrate would treat its children as precious commodities, but if we look deeper we would find this is not the case; that is, these young people are not receiving the response from life that they seek. That is why they cannot sit still until they find themselves.

## To Love is a Demanding Affair

It is sweet of people to say "I love you" or "I love you so much," but to love is actually difficult. There are times when a parent who does everything for the child ends up impairing the child's growth. Unless one steps back and allows life to happen, it is not true affection. Of course, if your child is in danger of being run over by a car or falling off a cliff, you must extend a hand to pull them out of danger. However, if there is a little bump in the road, there is no reason to take your child's hand to guide them around it. It is better to let them experience walking for themselves, even if it means taking a tumble now and then.

In this situation it is dangerous to say "I have to do this for the children." This is often just the parents' smug self-satisfaction talking. It might be a bit trying on the parents to be patient and to watch and wait, but this is because the parents themselves were brought up in an age of affluence when they did not have to wait around for results. This has led to the phenomenon of so-called monster or toxic parents who constantly voice their grievances to their children's teachers. I have heard from teachers that, more than the children, it is handling the parents that is the main cause of their occupational stress, and there are more than a few who have become clinically depressed from the ordeal.

In this age we have lost sight of the individual roles we play in the makeup of society. The cause of this imbalance actually lies in the period in which our present generation of parents grew up. It was a society of relative prosperity where, without much planning, you could get a job if you had marketable skills. As a result, living the good life, a life of affluence, is the only thing that they are conscious of; all other considerations have dropped away as they make their way through today's world.

## Not Knowing How to Greet Others

One comment I often hear is that children these days don't know how to greet people properly. I would say that is because they have never seen their parents do it. People who live in apartments are completely cut off from one another. They have few chances to exchange greetings with their neighbors. Also, with the nuclear family as the basic family pattern, the number of visitors is few.

It might not be that such families do not have guests, but that rather they do not invite guests that require formal greetings. To live such a life is free, convenient, individualistic, and avoids the onerous problem of formal greetings. The other side of that life is that children grow up with no exposure to the basic patterns of social life. Parents complain to the schools to teach their children the formal greetings, which is a complete turnabout of the way it used to be.

In temple family life, we often receive guests in a room where everyone sits on cushions. I have seen young people freeze in their tracks at the sight of the sitting room. It is not that they do not make any greeting at all. They want to but do not know how. When they enter from the hallway to the sitting room, they do not know that the proper way is to seat themselves first and then make the greeting. You cannot blame them since the homes they grew up in did not have the hallways or sitting rooms of a temple.

Since young people virtually without exception grow up in Western-style houses, the majority of them think that the correct way of greeting people is done standing up. I had one college student at a meeting in the sitting room who would get up to introduce himself every time someone came in. That was what he thought was the proper way of greeting someone.

I have heard that it is not until high school or college when students get a part-time job that they first learn how to do formal greetings. It would seem that until then they have no social situation where they need to use respectful etiquette. Parents think it is alright this way.

This is not to point a finger at others. I, too, had a lot of trouble with formal greetings. When I was a high school student living in a dormitory in Tokyo, I was even scolded about it once. When my father was asked by someone if he had taught me how to make a greeting when I was younger, he said that he had done that. But I knew that actually he had not done that. I was embarrassed. I remember thinking how different a parent and child can be in this respect. It could be that a parent intends to teach their child, and yet it does not get across. I remember learning a valuable lesson from that experience.

There are some people who think we should return to the system where the father is the head of the family and he raises his children strictly. However, the solution is not simple. Today the typical father does not know what the future holds and lives in uncertainty. This is not a situation where "father knows best."

To get into a good company, you have to go to a good school. To get into a good school, you have to get good grades. And so from the time you are little, as soon as possible you are made to learn the language you need, how to speak English, how to do mathematics, all of these things hastily decided for you by parents who want you to get ahead in life. In their hopes of an affluent life for their children, they put them on a busy schedule, always worried that their child might fall out of the running.

Here we see the scenario of parents trying to live through the achievements of their children. It is the desire of the parents that is being revealed through their children.

First, we have to correct the idea that the basis for living the good life, the life of affluence, is the only thing that we should pursue.

As a remedy to this, in Buddhism there is the "all sentient beings" way of thinking.

## What is This Phrase "All Sentient Beings"?

What do we mean by "all sentient beings"? In Buddhism, it is said that the Buddha's compassion is directed to "all sentient beings," that is, the collective existence of all living beings.

In my *Rescript* I stated that, "One thing we can sense from the Buddhist idea of the collective existence of all living beings is the extreme degree to which our human-centered culture has developed."

"All sentient beings" is the totality of all living beings that are alive. From our perch in modern life it is extremely difficult for us to imagine what this means.

The basis of Buddhism is the suffering of the individual. It is I as an individual who is saved; it is I as an individual who attains or receives enlightenment. The most basic thing is to solve the problem of my own life.

How am I to understand my life? First, beginning with the question of my so-called life, with this question our range of vision naturally expands to include all living things connected with my life. The most basic thing is to solve the suffering of my own life.

These living things are naturally countless in number. For that reason, beyond myself, beyond the people in my life, it is important to recognize the various life forms that exist. It is here that the term "all sentient beings," that is, the collective existence of all living beings, comes to bear.

The meaning of the original Sanskrit for "all sentient beings" is "living things, things that exist."

In India this term was used to indicate animals, but depending on the history and the locale, this gradually changed. When Buddhism was transmitted from China to Japan, it was widely understood to mean the totality of living things endowed with life.

When the phrase "living things" is used in talks on Jodo Shinshu, while it is often used to mean people or human beings, the usual emphasis is on the totality of all living things. If we inquire further, we come across the phrase "the beings that have transmigrated in countless lives." It means the interweaving of the lives of countless beings lost in delusion and repeatedly born and dying in transmigration.

This indicates a point of awareness where we become conscious of the transmigration of countless beings not merely coexisting with us on the same plane in physical terms, but also linked to us temporally over a vast period of time up to the present moment.

While this might differ from the space-time continuum that physics talks about, when we inquire into the source of our life, we find that space and time cannot be separated, and that it spreads back infinitely.

In temporal terms our life is represented symbolically by the transmigration along the six realms of existence, but we must not be overly concerned with this depiction. More important than knowing that there is a Buddhist word for living things is to discover this "living thing" aspect in yourself, that is, it is important to discover yourself as existing among all sentient beings.

## To Be "Here" in the Great Interconnectedness of Existence

To be alive among all sentient beings, that is, the collective existence of all living beings, does not only mean to be among the living things of the same period of time; it means that our life is connected all the way back; it is a life that has been repeated as it came down to us. Our life is not limited to this present place, and if we inquire as to its destiny, we can say that there is a life after this world to consider.

When we consider the present moment in the light of all sentient beings, we cannot allow the idea of man as the absolute measure of all things. It is not permissible that only people who are alive now should enjoy the good life. We cannot think of the present moment in such narrow terms. There is also a "now" that exists within the great interconnectedness of all living things.

If it is difficult to conceive of time and space in such broad terms, we might then think first of the support that we receive from the life existing around us in the same period of time. It is because we mutually support each other that this "I" who exists, is able to come into being. We should also come to know from this that we share the responsibility within a mutual relationship.

First of all, let us consider the relationship of mutual support among our human companions. Starting with our family and friends, we can expand our perception to take in the vast network of mutual support in our community, our society, our nation, and the earth as a whole.

Extending even further, we are mutually supported by the network of animal and plant life. Once we understand that, our world view then can broaden to appreciate the air and water on which all our lives depend.

All this begins from knowing the expression "sentient beings."

It is a key to opening up the vast network of mutual support. Once we become aware of the broad sphere of mutual ties we have to one another, we have to strongly question whether it is right for me to greedily indulge myself. To indulge oneself is not so much what others are doing; it comes down to the problem of what I, as a living being, am doing. If we reject the idea of being one with the totality of living things, all we see before us is the human-centered way of life where the words individuality and affluence loom large, but are in fact nothing but the narrowest of terms.

## The Question That Life Asks Us

Well, then, what is life?

I use this word all the time, and so it is not to point the finger at others when I say that it is often misused.

Once a word is misused, it is hard to consider its deeper implications. When someone starts to talk about things such as the grandeur of life, well, we simply pass it over.

When we speak of life, scientifically speaking, the word has several definitions. There is the life sustained by our metabolism, there is the life left to our children and our children's children, and so on, with a clear-cut division made between self and other. In contrast, there is the life of the earth as a whole, what scientists call Gaia. It might be too much to say that the earth is life, but what we mean by earth is not the planet per se but its closeness to life in terms of the life systems of the animals and plants that inhabit it.

In the scientific field, it becomes difficult to talk about life because different definitions of it abound. When the word life is used, you have to define your range of usage and the assumptions underlying your viewpoint.

Well, then, what is meant by me or myself?

We just talked about the peculiar set of circumstances leading young people to set out to "find themselves." What happens when we once again examine the problem not from the individual standpoint of me and myself, but from that of the plurality of living things? When that is done, we sense no resistance. Where, then, has our real self, that self we were so sure of, gone?

Our physical existence, if we take a close look at it to establish its existence, begins with the chromosomes inherited from our parents. These are supplied with nutrients from the outside world, containing protein and other necessary materials. For example, our skin cells must renew themselves, replacing themselves completely every few years.

With respect to the mind, regarding our intellect, preferences, and memories, virtually all of them are introduced from the world outside. We might pride ourselves on our good taste, but our makeup almost entirely derives from the outside. If we look back to the time when we were born, the only place that this me of mine existed was in the conversations between my parents and their friends.

If we start off with only a fuzzy image of the self in mind when we start to explain what the self is, we might be inclined to think that the self is at least not like a pile of sand whose particles will not adhere to one another. We have an image of a distinct body composed of parts that are completely cohesive. However, when we look for that self that holds everything together and try to extract it, every element of the self extends beyond the framework and connects to the world. We get an image of countless points of connection wherein the self equals the I. If all the connecting points were pulled from this so-called I, it would cease to exist that very instant. Thus this I of mine is not central to our existence.

Historically, in Western culture the individual self has been emphasized. In this way of thinking, there is an individual, therefore there is a society. In Buddhism, however, the individual exists because society exists; because there is the total interrelationship of all living beings, that the I that I am comes into existence. This is the Buddhist world view. It is a world view completely separate from the human-centered way of thinking.

There is another Buddhist expression, "the living beings existing in every direction (north, east, south, and west, plus the four intermediate directions, and zenith and nadir)." Let your thoughts resonate with this concept of the living beings existing in every direction, and I am sure it will reveal to you a vista entirely different from the Western world view which places the individual at the heart of its human-centered way of life.

## Switching Off Our Human-Centeredness

When this "all sentient beings" way of thinking becomes our focus, it makes us realize how modern culture is altogether too human-centered and too individualistic. It is a major problem when people perceive themselves as individualized units and lose sight of the connections that exist between them.

Every thing that exists external to themselves they regard as things existing just for their own personal use. These external objects appear to exist for their use. Wherever people go, all things external to them become goods for their consumption.

Technologically advanced countries eye the natural resources of developing countries for their use, and humanity as a whole sees plant and animal life, as well as minerals, only as natural resources. The environmental problem, which has worsened in recent years, is viewed solely from a European perspective, and as such is unable to go beyond its own limited outlook. That is because even the call for a sustainable economy is based on the goal of sustaining the human life style at all cost. I believe that it is possible for the "all sentient beings" way of thinking to bring about a great change in our human-centered way of thinking.

In the West, human beings are regarded as the most evolved species among all living creatures, and so it is only natural that the responsibility for the management of all species should fall on their shoulders. Though we might feel inclined to agree with this view, the reality is that humans do not manage their assumed role responsibly. They should be taking into consideration the lives of all living things equally; what we see, however, is people attempting to manage the world so that it works to their distinct advantage.

Some time ago in the West, when the discussion of the environmental problem had just begun, it was criticized by some who claimed that, in Christianity, God created man and gave him dominion over the natural world to use as he pleases. It may be this assumption that leads some to assert in more recent years that people are doing a responsible job of managing the natural world.

Because people are the managers does not mean they have free license to do whatever they wish. They have to accept full responsibility for looking after the welfare of the natural world.

However, as long as humans assume a privileged status, they can never apprehend the totality of living things, the plane where living things exist in every direction. That is because the word "management" holds the assumption that man must manage the world to humanity's particular advantage.

## People Live for Their Advantage Alone

Out of the impasse in which the fundamental Western approach had arrived, it was necessary to make a major shift in emphasis from Western culture as a tool for reworking nature to a culture that co-exists with nature. Among the catalysts cited for this change were the Buddhist views that "every living thing possesses Buddha nature" and "the mountain and the river, the grasses and the trees all become Buddha." However, the problem is not so simple.

Even if we follow such Buddhist thought and say that "every living thing there is, the mountain and the river, the grasses and the trees, all of them are equal," how does this match with the way we live?

The human species lives an existence that, from the very start, misses the mark when it comes to co-existence. This is a vital point that we should not fail to recognize. It is extremely difficult for people to accommodate a way of life that follows the "every living thing there is" principle. A fly comes buzzing into the room and either we swat it or chase it out. Here again we see a person acting to his personal advantage. There is no way anyone can live without thinking of what works to his advantage. Even so, if in some remote corner of someone's mind there is the idea of "all sentient beings," that is, the collective existence of all living beings, that reminds us that we cannot live with ourselves as the center.

A point of view has now emerged for critically viewing the way we live. Our way of life becomes modified by the thought, "Well, there is the 'all sentient beings' point of view to consider." Now, will this work to stop our good person in his tracks? Unless it does so, there is no stopping the mad spree on which we humans have launched ourselves.

The idea of all sentient beings, that is, the collective existence of all living beings, is not a principle or rule per se. There is the *"all sentient beings"* way of life, and there is the *Well, there is the "all sentient beings" point of view to consider* way of life. Some things become possible with one that are not possible with the other. If one seeks to live as a human being, it is not possible to concern ourselves with the fate of all sentient beings. It is not possible for us to live accommodating all forms of life and treating each of them as perfect equals. However, it can make us think, *Well, there is the "all sentient beings" point of view to consider, and this is the best that I can do for now*. More than this being a thought, this is our sense of the problem and it gives birth to a feeling of restraint on our part. This thinking is fundamentally different from the way of thinking that all things external to humans are tools for our use and that people are entitled to have control over them.

## There is Nothing but Artificiality in City Life

As the wielders of the powerful tool of scientific technology, it is of utmost importance, is it not, for us to have an awareness that there is a limit in putting every thing there is equal to human beings.

With a push of the switch, the air conditioner comes on, and in summer it is cool, in winter it is warm. What does this way of life usher in? Environment and ecology have become buzz words in today's world, and technology has endeavored to make devices with minimal ecological impact. That is all fine and good, but one aspect of it is that it is being taken advantage of to produce a new wave of consumer goods, showing just how difficult it is to make a qualitative move away from our ingrained human-centered way of thinking.

There are many hurdles we have to overcome if we are to put the Buddhist view of "all sentient beings," that is, the collective existence of all living beings, in the center of our lives. This is not just talk; rather, it is important that we have a real sense of "all sentient beings" in the context of our everyday life.

The heart of the Tokyo metropolitan district has been made over to man's every advantage. When you stand there surrounded by those huge skyscrapers, it is hard to get a sense of all sentient beings. Thanks to the softening of building codes, Tokyo has become a huge megalopolis on a scale that cannot be compared with the city I once knew in my student days. It could be that pollution has decreased, but I also sense that the natural open spaces have been dramatically reduced. Virtually all of it has been made over into artificial settings where people are living. The good earth and her rivers are paved over with concrete and asphalt.

The only animals we come across are pets. The plants we see are potted ones or the ones that were planted in the park, all of them bought and sold items. All the other plants that once were there have been removed.

The crows are not regarded as birds but as pests, the insects are seen as harmful and the plants as weeds to be eliminated. The pesky crows and the harmful insects are only so because humans have upset the balance of nature, causing them to swell in number.

With the urbanization of these areas, there is growing concern over the so-called heat island phenomenon. There are also other important issues to be addressed such as the problem of commercialism and the lack of contact with nature.

Fortunately, in the Hongwanji in which I live, there are insects, a family of badgers has made it their home, and birds come flying in. Once you live this kind of life, you can truly sense the mystery of "all sentient beings." There is many an insect that is not to our personal advantage to have. However, with the advance of the seasons, the flowers bloom, the insects call, and the birds come to roost. With this alone we can live our everyday life sensing the mystery of nature.

## What Retirement Might Mean For Us

For those of us who are living in artificial dwellings due to economic necessity, I wonder if it is possible to make a small change in our lives. Right now a lot of baby boomers are reaching retirement age, and many of them are seeking to retire to live in the countryside. No doubt many of them have become weary of the tedious productivity-oriented life of the cities.

Though some may have regrets when leaving their careers behind, retirement also might offer them an opportunity to get a new focus in life.

People now regularly live into their eighties and since this means an extension of the years after retirement, how to plan to live out these years is a theme often discussed. Since we are fortunate to live this long, it is important that we once again reassess the sense of values we have held up to now.

In that sense Buddhism has no age when to start. Sakyamuni Buddha was twenty-nine when he left his home and began ascetic practice. Shinran Shonin was nine when he left his home behind for monastic life and was twenty-nine when he reached a major turning point in his life. It is important to take the opportunity when it arises to introduce a change in our lives. For example, up to now older people have been too busy working, but when retired, if they have the time and the spiritual freedom to do so, should take the time once again to look at their lives in a new light. It is never too late to do so.

Now even if I worked in a huge building, it would be most unusual if I knew what mountain was leveled as the source of the sand used in the concrete. When we live in the midst of this man-made artifice, however, how can we possibly have a real sense of nature? It is for that reason it is necessary to look back and reassess our life.

Leave behind the masses of people living in huge buildings, and if possible, find a way of life where you have some contact with nature. You don't have to dedicate your entire week to do this, half a day or an hour will do. At that time, put your mind in touch with the plants and animals, with nature.

Ask yourself what has caused you to be as you are. We have already said that it is because all sentient beings exist, therefore I am that I am. If we restate this as a Pure Land Buddhist teaching, it would be the insight that "I receive, therefore I am."

This does not mean that I have received some particular thing. My existence, the I who I am, is what I have received.

## What an Obutsudan (Buddha's Shrine) Can Do For Your Everyday Life

It might seem a bit abrupt to ask but, do you have an Obutsudan in your house? Have you ever made offerings to the shrine? It seems that there are many families that do not have an Obutsudan these days. It does not matter if it is a small and simple one. I hope you will consider having an Obutsudan in your home. Having one provides an opportunity to look back on the day, to think about the way you are living, and this is most important.

If there is a place where you can place your hands together in *gassho*, then there is a place in your everyday life where you can think. And symbolic of this is the act of *Osanae*, where the *Obuppan* (offering of rice) is placed on the Obutsudan.

Our lives everyday are founded upon the meals that we partake. Rice is the main staple that the Japanese people cannot get by without. Before partaking of that meal, rice is symbolically offered to the Buddha as Osanae. It is a way to go beyond simply eating when hungry.

When you travel in the rich farming areas like Niigata, there were once wealthy farmers called *gono* who lived on large estates with wide *zashiki* (a formal Japanese room) that rivaled those of the smaller temples in the city. Here, historically, the peasant farmers who worked the land would gather to hold services and to listen to sermons. However, many of these peasants were impoverished and it was not easy for them to offer the Obuppan of rice. And so during the Edo period (1603-1867), millet might have been offered as the Obuppan.

The kind of rice that will adhere when piled up is a certain kind of rice. It is not possible to do this with the long grain rice of Southeast Asia. Even though it is called Osanae, the only thing that can be done is to put the rice on a plate.

It is unclear when the tradition of eating white rice started, and the tradition of rice as a staple has long been discussed. However, since it has come down to us in this way, I think it important to preserve this tradition. These matters seem meaningless when you think of them in practical terms, but they have something valuable lodged within them.

When you approach the Obutsudan, when you Osanae the Obtsudan, you put your hands together. That form, that posture you assume, is an important one. You are affirming the place on which you are standing, you are setting the attitude with which you will meet the world, and there is great meaning to internalizing the Buddhist sense of values.

## A Life For All Seasons

Where does the rice we are eating come from? City dwellers have no idea. All they know is that rice is sold in the shops. However, when you give rice a place in your life as Osanae, it is no longer something that money can buy. Now we see that this is something we receive—this facet of life we become keenly aware of, and this keen awareness of ours is important. It is a little different from a "Yes, I understand" response where our business-like attitude toward life is at work.

When children say *Itadakimasu* (let us humbly partake this our daily meal) before eating their school lunches, some parents protested, saying that since they had paid the lunch fee out of their own pockets, why is it necessary for their children to say that. It is indeed true that one can buy rice with money. However, we are not paying the money directly to the rice; we are paying to cover the costs incurred by the people who mediated the process of growing the rice.

This is true for the rice and fish we eat. When it comes to their lives, there is no way that money can compensate them. It is important to be aware that there are things that cannot be purchased with cash.

Long ago, when my son was in kindergarten, we went to Shiga Prefecture by car. Stopping at a rest area along the way, we all got out to take a look. The rice had just been planted and the fields of green shoots waved back and forth in the wind. It was beautiful.

I asked my son, "Do you know what that is?"

"A golf course?" was his answer.

I was rather shocked by his response and thought I need to take him to see some rice fields right away. Later, I was able to have him experience planting rice shoots for himself.

Japan has four seasons, and even though the routines of life still change with the seasons, people are losing the essence of that way of life and the opportunity to sense the transformations. To experience as little change as possible and to resist any kind of change, are now typical of urban planning.

When Japan changed from an agricultural society to an urban and industrial one, some Buddhist scholars believed that the Buddhist message lost some of its meaning.

Seeds are planted, shoots come up, seedlings are replanted, flowers blossom, become fruit, and the stage is set for the next cycle of life. This is nature.

I have planted many plants and flowers. Recently, though, once they flower, that is the end; it is not possible to obtain seeds from them to plant again. This is true even in the case of vegetables. People no longer think to gather the seeds after the daikon or carrots bloom. The commercial varieties are designed so as to make it impossible to obtain seeds. The argument is that the seed companies cannot profit enough if this were the case. Economics have impacted even the seed germ.

In the idea of "all sentient beings," that is, the collective existence of all living beings, it is now difficult to see that all things are connected as sentient beings. In such a time as this, we wish to restore the sense of life as being a gift we receive.

Toward that end, as we sit facing the Obutsudan, we first have to be aware of this problem, and make the time to look back on our lives as part of our daily routine. In the course of doing this, we no longer have to be overtly conscious of it as we have become keenly aware of "all sentient beings."

In the next chapter, we will discuss things having limits, and will reflect more on the matter of limitations. This is an important point that is related to what Buddhism calls *klesa*, our blind passions.

Chapter 3

# Man is Bound to Die

*To go there is easy,*
*and yet no one is there.*
*—The Sutra of Immeasurable Life*

## As the Bell Tolls Solemnly at the End of the Year

While society undergoes massive changes, there are some things that never change. In the timeless pattern of temple life, there is the solemn tolling of the bell at year's end. It is at this time, once a year, that a great many Japanese people feel they are Buddhist, if only for a moment. As they listen to the tolling of the temple bell, these year-end Buddhists of ours are moved by the sound, and think to themselves, "Ah, there goes another year!" Every year, the tolling of the bell brings the year to a close. And yet there is something deeply moving about it.

At year's end the bell is struck one hundred and eight times. The number is symbolic of the number of *bonno*, or blind passions (Sanskrit, klesa) that afflict man. The sound of the bell brings the existence of these bonno to our attention in an attempt to strike them away. However, it is incorrect to think we have been purged of these tendencies simply because we heard the bell ring one hundred and eight times.

Since we have brought up the subject of bonno, what exactly do we mean by the term and what do we mean to realize them? Let us give the matter some serious thought.

The implications that bonno hold for man are quite complex, and so bonno is not easy to explain. If we were to attempt to list all the bonno that pertain to us, it would be far more than the symbolic one hundred and eight. These bonno lead us by the nose in every imaginable facet of our lives.

In a nutshell, bonno is bound to the problem of our limitations.

There is a limit to our lifespans, there is a limit to our knowledge, and there is a limit to our physical abilities. No matter how eager and capable one might be, our existence is defined by our limitations. It is a source of frustration and pain that we cannot step beyond these limitations.

If we were asked to enumerate all of our limitations, it is not something that we could do. That is why in every age we hear the words of triumphant spiritualism proclaiming, there is nothing you cannot do if you put your mind to it, or that the only reason you cannot do it is you do not try. This sort of triumphant spiritualism might be effective when encouraging someone, but by and large it is useless.

There is a limit to our lifespans. This is understood to mean that everyone has to die sometime. However, the hardest thing to do is to wake up to the fact that the life I am living is limited. An immense gap exists between our limitations in a general sense and the limitations of each and every one of us as individuals. That is because even though our lifespans are limited, is there anyone who does not hate to think that they one day must die?

These bonno inevitably prevent true self knowledge. They appear when we do not clearly realize these limitations as our own. The hardest thing for people to do is to admit their own limitations, and Buddhism has long pointed this out through the use of the term bonno. If it were possible to have a clear awareness of our limitations, this would lead to the world of awakening or liberation.

## This Body is Born to Undergo Illness, Old Age, and Death

Once I had a dialogue with the anatomist Takeshi Yoro (*b.* 1937) who told me, "A priest has to clearly tell people that they are bound to die." His words left a strong impression on me. Rather than say harmless and inoffensive things to console and heal the listener, you must say the truth, however much it hurts: that is the role of a priest. I remember nodding in agreement when I heard this.

In Japan, when a person is dying, people encourage them, "*Ganbatte!* Keep holding on!" They say words to console and heal them, as if we will all be going to the spa once they get better. In Southeast Asia, when someone is sick and facing death, or when a family has lost a member, the priests will tell them that a body is born into a life of illness, old age, and death. In short, man is bound to die.

In Japan, during a funeral, if a priest were to say that it is man's fate to die, it would not go down well. Priests are obliged to say words of consolation. However, in this situation, it has traditionally been the role of Buddhism to remind people there is no way a man will escape death.

The Buddhist funeral is a representative case, but there are many other situations where it is clear that modern life averts its eyes from death. Another example is the graveyard.

There are records from the Heian period regarding burial practices. However, such graves were reserved for the influential members of society. It is not clear how the common people disposed of their dead.

Cremation is now standard, but up until the mid-fifties burial was still quite common. These days, however, people talk about how important it is to have one's own grave and what it means to have an ancestral grave, as if this practice extended back to ancient times.

Since ancient times, in areas with high population density, there were disposal sites for bodies. The author Masao Suzuki (*b.* 1926) wrote a book called, *The Town of Edo is Littered with Bones*. Such disposal sites are still found in the middle of large cities like Tokyo. It does not take long to dig up bones buried just below the surface.

Many elementary schools in Tokyo are built upon temple sites that were torn down during the *haibutsu kishaku* "down with Buddhism" movement in the 19th century during the Meiji period. When any construction on these school grounds is necessary, an excavation will often turn up bones. The Adashino area in Kyoto, where the Nenbutsuji is located, was also such a cremation site and burial ground. Here we get a glimpse of what is only natural for a place with so many deaths and bodies to dispose of.

## Death Has Been Banished From Our Cities

Now, however, in cities like Tokyo and Kyoto there is no place where we come across the dead. What was once a common occurrence is now gone. Once corpses are no longer there, it becomes difficult for us to think of death as familiar. The cremation site has been cleaned up and made brighter. Some say it looks more like a hotel than a cremation site. At any rate, modern life tries not to look at death or think about death. All these aspects of our modern cities have been sanitized.

Earlier we talked about the baby boomers reaching retirement age. Among retirees in Japan, there are many who become *Ohenro-san*, pilgrims, and I have heard that there are quite a number who make the rounds of pilgrimage sites. One especially popular route is the 88-temple Shikoku pilgrimage. It seems that this is a form of leisure or a journey of self-discovery.

However, in the past, one did not become an *Ohenro-san* in this way. Those who set out on pilgrimage were burdened with problems and worries for which they were desperately seeking a solution. During the Edo period, some of the pilgrims were those who were seriously ill and set out looking for a place to die. Even today there are a few who set off with this serious frame of mind.

If one sets off on a pilgrimage with a tourist's frame of mind, there is no opportunity to think seriously about the problem that death poses. Thus, it is almost impossible for people today to think about the implications of their bonno.

Everyone knows that there is a limit to how long people will live; no one knows whether they will live to be fifty or eighty years old. Just saying that the human lifespan has its limit does not connect us to the question of what we should be doing about it.

And so people deadlocked in their bonno are troubled. These troubled feelings are tangled up with the fierce desire to live. To say these desires are bad, though, says nothing and gives us nowhere to go.

## There is No Dividing Good From Evil

When a mother loses her child, she is distraught. How much she had hoped to raise that little one and watch her grow! There are some, though, who would contend that such feelings are a form of desire. However, I would question whether it is possible to simply say that they are bad and should be dispensed with. It would be rather cruel of us to have to tell our bereaved mother to stop feeling sad and put her grief behind her. It is as if we were saying, that's your problem, it has nothing to do with me.

It is wrong to take another's life. On the field of battle, however, where others threaten to take your life, you are forced to act. One has to defend one's life and those of one's fellow soldiers. There are some who would contend, though, that this is a form of bonno, and that we are merely acting out of our desire to live. On the other hand, there are those who would say that the soldier who does not discharge his weapon on the field of battle is in the wrong.

This example might be extreme, but I think it goes to show that, depending on situations and conditions, there is no way for us to know how we ought to think or act. When we do not dismiss the problem, saying it has nothing to do with me, and think of what bonno implies *for me*, we run straight into a gray area where even those acts that are said to grow out of our desires cannot simply be dismissed as wrong. It is impossible to say that this is good and that is bad. As a result, we end up living in that gray area where it is impossible for us to say conclusively that I will live my life by choosing what is right and abandoning what is wrong.

Shinran Shonin is said to have stated, "I know nothing at all of good or evil." (Postscript, *A Record in Lament of Divergences*, second edition, p. 42) As a comment on our personal situations, those who cannot tell good from evil and live deep in the shadows of this gray area are called foolish beings of karmic evil caught in birth-and-death (ibid., p. 41).

The words "karmic evil" in the following phrase "a foolish being of karmic evil caught in birth-and-death," gives us an important insight to understanding what bonno means. Awakening to this karmic evil is an important pillar in the teaching of Shinran Shonin. This message, however, is one that has not yet gotten through to the modern world. This particular message might be the most difficult one for modern society to grasp.

Even if people are told to "awaken to this worst kind of karma," they have no idea what was said to them and may feel like laughing. How then are we to understand karmic evil?

Karmic evil, in the teaching of Jodo Shinshu, varies in content and depends on the individual and their situation. Throughout life, people have to take the lives of other living things. They must do this in order to eat. If one thinks of it in this way, this is karmic evil.

In our relationships with others, we do and say things that unintentionally hurt. Concerning human ethics, this is karmic evil. When a crime is committed and the law is broken, this too is karmic evil.

Those who have come to a serious understanding of this teaching will say that if you doubt Amida Buddha's Sincere (True Real) compassion or doubt your impending liberation, that is karmic evil. There are even some who would insist that this latter case is truly the epitome of karmic evil, compared to which our worldly infractions are nothing.

## What Shinran Shonin Teaches Regarding Karmic Evil

In this way, there are many facets when viewing karmic evil. Shinran Shonin teaches that "karmic evil" and our awareness of "karmic evil" have two levels of meaning.

The first is karmic evil as the criterion for realizing Suchness (True and Real) coming to our rescue.

In one work Shinran Shonin wrote that, "Foolish beings (as expressed in the parable of the two rivers of water and fire) are full of ignorance and blind passion. Our desires are countless, and anger, wrath, jealousy, and envy are overwhelming, arising without pause; to the very last moment of life they do not cease, or disappear, or exhaust themselves." (*Notes on Once-Calling and Many-Calling*, *CWS*, pp. 487-488)

That is, to be filled with bonno is to be one who is unable to control their many desires, their anger, wrath, and jealousy until the moment they die: this is what characterizes the ordinary person. I am completely sure I am just an ordinary person. Awaken to the foolish nature of your self, that is what Shinran Shonin is saying to us.

The one problem that I just cannot seem to resolve on my own is this karmic evil. As I am just an ordinary person who cannot live without clinging to this karmic evil, this serves as a guideline for my liberation.

The second level of meaning is karmic evil as an admonishment to fellow seekers.

In a letter to one fellow seeker, Shinran Shonin admonished him with the following words, "It is indeed sorrowful to give way to impulses with the excuse that one is by nature possessed of blind passions—excusing acts that should not be committed, words that should not be said, and thoughts that should not be harbored—and to say that one may follow one's desires in any way whatever." (*Lamp for the Latter Ages*, *CWS, I*, p. 553)

With regard to a fellow seeker who let himself do whatever his heart desired, Shinran Shonin set down ethical guidelines, saying that he must awaken to the worst kind of karma that is fueling his behavior. As Shinran Shonin explained, it is only through awakening to karmic evil's hold over us that it is possible to curb inappropriate actions.

In either case, karmic evils originate within each individual and there is no getting rid of them or reforming them.

## Awakening and Liberation Are Two Sides of the Same Coin

There is a simple side to our bonno. Once I noticed the words, "Awaken to your foolish self..."posted on the bulletin board of the Zojoji temple in Tokyo. It was in the opening line of the Jodoshu's *Declaration for the Twenty-first Century*. I also saw the same words posted at the Jodoshu's Chion-in headquarters in Kyoto. This sentiment, "to awaken to our foolish self," is found not only in the writings of Honen Shonin, the founder of Jodoshu, but is also part of the legacy inherited by his disciple Shinran Shonin.

In a letter, Shinran Shonin wrote, "Persons of the Pure Land tradition attain birth in the Pure Land by becoming their foolish selves" (*Lamp for the Latter Ages, CWS, I,* p. 531). This refers to a form of awakening arrived at through recognizing our foolish self.

The more we are awakened to our natural state, the more we have to confess our foolish selves. Our liberation takes place when, at the moment we are drawn to this insight, we profoundly awaken to the fact that we have been supported by Buddha's Sincerity (True and Real) all along.

Moreover, our liberation has come about by the very fact that we cling to our bonno.

There are two aspects to this event: there is the element of our critical awakening to the fact that we cling to our bonno, and there is the fact of our bonno determining our mode of liberation. Thus awakening and liberation go hand in hand.

In concrete terms, at what point do we take notice of our "foolish self full of blind passions," you ask. What must we do to open up that pathway?

As a guide to opening up this side of us, I have coined the phrase, "Living in the teeth of life," literally, "living in earnest." A person who seeks to live in the teeth of life is one who sees life not as someone else's business but as a challenge which one must earnestly accept as one's own.

## What an Evil Person Is

Another important phrase in Jodo Shinshu is "the evil person." It ranks alongside "a foolish being" and "foolish self."

The following famous saying is attributed to Shinran Shonin: "Even a good person attains birth in the Pure Land, so it goes without saying that an evil person will. Though it is so, people commonly say, 'Even an evil person attains birth, so it goes without saying that a good person will.'" (*A Record in Lament of Divergences*, second edition, p. 7)

In other words, if it is possible for the good to be born in the Pure Land, then it stands to reason that a bad person would attain birth without question. While this is the Pure Land rationale, worldly opinion would argue quite the opposite: that if it is possible for an evil person to be born in the Pure Land, then it stands to reason that a good person would attain birth without question.

Here, an "evil person" refers to a person who lacks the capacity and qualities to make a Buddha out of himself through his own efforts.

Since this particular phrase has impact, a question that is often asked is, "How then is it possible for an evil person to be liberated?" Sometimes people will ask, "What about a person who has killed or hurt many people?" The phrase, "evil person" is easily associated with the person who has committed crimes, and so the problem of crime is an important theme in Jodo Shinshu.

Behind the question of the person who commits crimes, though, there lurks the thinking that the person who commits crimes has nothing to do with me, it is none of my business, and it is this indifferent take on the issue that is the real problem. I will never become an evil person; an evil person is someone else, not me—this kind of thinking is the fundamental problem.

No one wants to think of themselves as a bad person. However, as long as we think of ourselves as standing on the side of the good and the righteous, as long as we are the ones who are in a position to judge, there will be many things we will encounter in life that will irk us and which we will find wholly objectionable; we will never be able to sit back and gaze upon the world with warmth and understanding. Anything that does not match up to our expectations will inconvenience us and we will hold others to blame.

Our critic may ask: What about the accused in a vicious murder case who has killed someone, who has injured someone that still cannot put the fearsome experience behind, who has caused the loss of someone precious that has left that person's family reeling in the wake of the crime—surely that person should be judged, without question!

Let us put our judgmental stance aside and think on the matter from another perspective. Can we decisively say that we are altogether different from that individual? Is that wretched fool of a person really so unrelated to me?

When it comes to an ordinary person subject to fits of anger, ill temper, and envy, there is no telling what such a fool of a person might do given the right circumstances. That is why only Buddha's Sincerity (True and Real) is capable of liberating each and every living being there is, without passing judgment on them.

It is only when we encounter this Buddha mind, that is wholly determined to work out our liberation, that it becomes possible for the axis of our understanding to shift and for us to then realize we have no other choice but to be liberated. At that moment it is possible for us to say there is a force in life that comes to the rescue of even those of bad karma like myself. This is not somebody else's business; this is an event that has happened to me on the very stage of living in the teeth of life, that is, living life in earnest.

## Self-Responsibility and Self-Justification

Human nature being what it is, however, it is rare for someone to shift their orientation to a sense of guilt over what they have done.

The phrase "self-responsibility" has recently been in vogue, but by and large, it is used to force someone else to take responsibility for themselves.

A person defending themselves with the words, "I did not have a choice," when countered with, "You did have a choice," will only glower and say, "Well, then, what should I have done?"

It could well be that people today do not want to consider awakening to their own sense of guilt. In court, a person accused of murder will do anything to defend himself. It is not legally to his advantage to show a deep sense of guilt.

Contemporary people have taken the criticism of others to

fever pitch, while not turning an eye to their own guilt. Rather than an emphasis on self-responsibility, self-justification has become prominent. This need to justify oneself seems to be a result of living in this age of uncertainty.

We want to wash our hands of everything and say, "Look, it has nothing to do with me." Even if we are told we should not let our thoughts get hung up like that, when we recall that someone had said something bad about us, it only makes us want to retreat even further into our shells. Trapped in this miserable state of affairs, it is highly unlikely we will ever reach that exit point called awakening.

## Seeking the Way of Living Earnestly, Living in the Teeth of Life

I believe Buddhism goes beyond the level of the individual. As Buddhists we must turn an eye to the broader problems afflicting society.

A while ago, the news carried a report that relief supplies sent to a disaster-stricken country were plundered. In 2007, the Peruvian earthquake caused widespread damage. A lack of food caused countries from around the world to send supplies. However, once the shipments arrived, they were plundered by looters.

There were many people who were upset to hear that the food supplies reached the disaster area but ended up in the hands of looters. However, when there is an earthquake in an area where there is a chronic shortage of food, the reality is that unless one plunders, one cannot live.

People watching the news cannot see deeply into the situation to know that foodstuffs are in insufficient supply. They do not see the poverty and hunger; they only criticize the fact that the supplies were plundered. This is the typical response of those who see the situation as someone else's problem.

When faced with a problem on a worldwide scale, people evade the issue by saying right off there is nothing we can do about it. Whatever problem arises, they chant, "The situation is hopeless!" Indeed, where do we draw the line between the situation is hopeless and it is our responsibility to take on the problem?

In 2004, when the Indonesia tsunami occurred, I heard that it was extremely difficult for relief efforts to reach the people in the affected areas. Since the social infrastructure, that we take for granted in our own country, was not in place, looting occurred on a daily basis. When bringing relief supplies to areas ruled by syndicates, the supplies will only end up with those who wield the most power.

It is necessary for the relief work to be protected by the military. There is no way to get the relief supplies only to those who are really in need without the help of the military. There are some who are absolutely opposed to the use of the military, but is there any other choice? There are places in the world where goodwill simply is not sufficient.

Africa, for instance, is like this. The United Nations will send shipments of food and medicine and one portion of it will end up with the powerful political dictator of that country. It is nearly impossible for the whole of it to reach the intended parties. The distribution of wealth in the world is badly skewed, and the majority of people live in abject poverty.

In the case of Africa, there were centuries of colonialism, and control of natural resources by the European countries. We cannot ignore these factors and think that goodwill will make up for everything. And so does this mean the ball is back in the court of our naysayers who claim the situation is hopeless?

Where do we draw the line and say it is none of our business?

So what must I do to accept the problem as my own? That is a difficult question, but this is nothing other than "living earnestly, living in the teeth of life." The problems of bonno and the worst kind of karma must each be contemplated in terms of our experiences in daily life, rather than through doctrinal interpretation—that is what living in the teeth of life, living earnestly, is all about. You can enter into this way of living from what you truly feel, in the shared experience of life where you can say, "Yes, I know that feeling."

Life never turns out the way we expect. Each time life takes an unexpected turn, we have the opportunity to revise our thinking and see ourselves in a new light, that is linked to our way of living in the teeth of life, living earnestly. It is not the attitude of those who say "that's somebody else's problem."

## The Cause of Awakening is Completed in Ordinary Life

For the first time the admonishment to live earnestly takes on great meaning, when you accept that man is bound to die. I have heard that when someone is ill and are told they have only a few months to live, the world around them suddenly becomes radiantly beautiful. Everyday things that they once passed by without noticing, all of a sudden take on new meaning as precious memories to cherish. When we become aware of our finitude, something clicks into focus.

If, when told you have cancer, someone were to say, well, you have lived long enough so it does not matter, surely that would make you upset. Even if it were true, it would be upsetting to be told that. Herein lies a problem.

Almost a kind of shock therapy, it is unsettling to find yourself involved in the process of dying. If someone were to suddenly tell you that you were about to die, there is no one, neither prince nor holy man, who could take the news calmly.

In the course of ordinary life it is important to consider death. On any given day, when we accept the fact that man is bound to die, though it will still come as a shock to learn it is your time, it is possible for you to keep it in check. It may upset you and yet you can watch it happening and say to yourself, "Why, of course I am upset, why shouldn't I be?"

There is a Jodo Shinshu saying: The cause for Awakening is completed in ordinary life (*heizei gojo*). When on any given day we let the truth of our coming Awakening define our lives, the moment of death no longer terrifies us. This is what these words of advice tell us. If on any given day you keep this thought in the corner of your mind, that man is bound to die, when that time comes, even though it may throw you for a loop and upset you greatly, putting you through changes, in the end it may well be that you will be able to come to terms with death and accept the fact of your dying.

## The Eighties Way of Dying

For those in their eighties, the big question of how I will die keeps bubbling up. For our generation, and for the baby-boomers who follow us, there is a feeling that we still have not lived enough. If that is the case, thinking about death for a baby-boomer is, in a sense, half someone else's business, so it is like listening in on a good preparatory seminar. There are some Buddhists who think that talking about death to those who are suffering from illness is meaningless, but I would contend that kind of thinking is a minority view.

A member of our denomination once told me that she was shocked by what her cousin told her. Her mother had been in good spirits one day and died suddenly on her way home. Her mother was of an advanced age, and so her cousin tried to console her by saying, "Your mother lived long enough and so it was good it happened this way." That might be so, and of course these words were meant to console her, but to hear someone say so was upsetting. When it is someone else's mother you might think of it this way, she said, but when it is your own mother, you cannot only say she lived long enough and be done with it.

"Man is born to die" is easy to understand, but hard to come to terms with.

People must accept that we must die, and though we can understand that if we must, we cannot accept this fact. Caught between these two poles, people wobble and stumble along through life—we must not fail to see this is how we are.

Modern man thinks himself clever and regards others as fools. As a result, even if he hears something of prime importance, the chances of it remaining on his mind on any given day are small.

## Taking Note of Things

We have talked about awakening to our bonno, awakening to our karmic evil, awakening to our finitude, as well as awakening to our foolish selves. An important point is that awakening and liberation are paired; one is a function of the other. It is from this understanding that I state in my *Rescript*: Through awakening to ourselves as ordinary people trapped in transmigration through and laden with karmic evil, there opens up a world of joy and gratitude.

The question now arises: how is it that, through awakening

to our ordinary man trapped in transmigration, joy is born in our hearts?

Shinran Shonin offers a clue, answering this question by stating, "Persons of the Pure Land tradition attain birth in the Pure Land by becoming their foolish selves." (*Lamp for the Latter Ages, CWS, I,* p. 531) I think that the process of returning referred to here can be said to be overlaid with the meaning of awakening.

*Zanki*, to feel hurt and ashamed, is the subject of many Jodo Shinshu sermons. If we hear only that much, we are left wondering how this can have any connection to the joy of encountering the teaching. Are we not simply being told that we are these worthless good-for-nothings and that's that? This hardly makes for a religious teaching, is the thought that flits across our minds.

Indeed, if we emphasize only the aspect of the statement, when you awaken to yourself as an ordinary man trapped in transmigration and laden with karmic evil, there opens up a world of joy and feeling, it is highly unlikely that we will ultimately arrive at this feeling of joy that was discovered by Honen Shonin and Shinran Shonin. We have to ask ourselves how and when this will be transformed into joy. How are we to take notice of things such that it truly becomes an occasion for joy?

Simply looking at events taking place within yourself is not enough. You must notice that you are being made to take notice of things by the working of something greater than yourself. Unless we do so, there is no true joy or gratitude forthcoming.

## The Joy of Realizing

It is important to recognize that Buddha's Sincerity (True and Real) is making us take notice of things.

You are standing before something that goes beyond your self.

That is, beyond your involvement in society, you are linked to something "other" that exists at a deeper level. This something other is inextricably bound up with you at the very root source of your existence.

Unless our hearts open up to Buddha's Sincerity (True and Real), no joy is forthcoming. A world previously unseen, now comes into view. That is, unless we realize a broader world view, there is no joy brought about in our hearts.

Regardless of the fact that our individual efforts alone can never make a Buddha out of us, our joy is found in receiving the working of the other; making a gift of buddhahood is the source of our joy.

At the same time, even though we have been given a confirmation of our eventual buddhahood, we are without the slightest feeling of joy. It is said that Buddha's Sincerity (True and Real) takes this into account and this should make us realize that the working of the other is altogether reliable in this respect. We might call this the joy that comes from being released from our narrow "joyless" world.

Though we might think we understood what was said, when we return to the world of daily life, it is nothing but the same old grind of suffering and worries all over again. The din of suffering is so overwhelming that we barely have a chance to hear ourselves think. When standing face to face with a real problem, all an ordinary human being can do is worry and fret.

Modern man knows we should ask ourselves big questions about the nature of life and death and Amida Buddha's sincere (True and Real) compassion, and yet when queried, we evade them and say we will get around to them. Whether we want to go to the Pure Land or have a Zen experience, well, the thought never occurred to us. Nor did the thought occur to us to be liberated by the Dharma. Caught in this state of suffering, somehow we can never seem to find the way leading to this dimension of joy.

We live our everyday lives as if swept along downstream. Sickness may make our golden years an uncertain affair, our family relations may have turned sour, our company might be restructuring and plan to give us the boot. We live with worries and uncertainty as our constant companions.

Whenever problems are encountered in the course of the day, most people lay the blame on someone else and do not think any further about it. They do not make this an opportunity to venture one step deeper into themselves. When a person is admonished to think more deeply, he or she is peeved to find they were the ones in the wrong, and if that is what Buddhism is about, well, who needs it!

If we are too afraid of the dark, we will never set out towards the world of light.

## The Dust Motes Dancing in the Sunlight

Religious joy takes various forms in people. The joy that I have experienced is not the kind where the world suddenly becomes bright like a light bulb went on. Instead, there is something that I have been made aware of that was previously hidden. It is the joy of having received the gift of wisdom and compassion working in my life. This was not a spectacular experience of joy. It was more like an experience that came oozing out slowly from the deep recesses of my heart.

Of course, it is wonderful if you have a spectacular experience, but if that does not take place, you can still experience what Jodo Shinshu calls shinjin. When the room is dark, you will not see the dust motes floating in the air. But throw open the curtains and let the light come flooding in, and the dust motes will appear.

No matter how hard we may try, it is difficult to notice things by our efforts alone. More than our taking notice, it is more often the case of our being made to take notice. Here the passive voice is important, that is, we are made to look at the situation from the opposite perspective. The active element in our awakening is Buddha's Sincerity (True and Real) that is making us take notice.

When a person is alive by virtue of receiving everything, that person notices that we all are being made to live. That person is made to notice that living itself is a function of receiving. That is why it is important for everyone to be aware that "man is born to die" and to awaken to their finitude.

Contemporary man thinks that life is the crystallization of his efforts alone. From the time we were small we were told to try hard to make something of ourselves. We were brought up thinking that success is a product of our own efforts. However, that is to arrive at an incorrect conclusion. Instead, it is important to see life from the broader perspective of our being made to live, where everything is causing us to live. Then we realize that we are being made to live. When we realize that we exist as the sum total of everything we have received, this then becomes a starting point for awakening to ourselves as ordinary people.

## Those Who Think Life is So Easy

It is typical of people to make an all-out effort to eliminate worries and uncertainties from our lives. Then, once we have eliminated our worries we should be content, should we not, but is this the case?

Have we really removed the root cause of our uncertainty?

In fact, we have not really solved the problem, we only act as if the problem is solved. We act as if life is easy when we take this approach and say, "Well, that's life!" We might even be letting life pass by us unnoticed. That might be a rather arrogant attitude toward life.

When we are ill, we go to the doctor for treatment. This is a typical way to deal with a problem. A young person might recover immediately, but as the years pile up the trips to the doctor become more frequent and we end up taking medication on a daily basis. This is not to say we should not be doing this. Just taking medication, however, does not solve the problem that our bodies are weakening with age and sickness.

When you find that you have a problem that you cannot solve, how do you react? When you notice this about yourself, you must turn around and face yourself just as you are; this is important.

It is not possible to become a person who never gets sick, and there are some kinds of sickness from which people will never get well. When they realize this, some people suddenly become religious or look for miracle cures. On the other hand, it never occurs to them to think, "Wait, I should turn to the Dharma!" There is something blocking the way. They seek a fast solution to their problems instead.

Health fads become popular for the same reason. There are even doctors who will come out and declare the fad to be sound. When we are swept up by these trends, it only avoids the real problem.

Because we do not arrive at an insight into our foolish selves, we are doomed to live like fools who are strangers to themselves.

Why do we never stop and question ourselves? Could it be that we are too busy to do so?

Once we hit rock bottom, it never occurs to us to ask what that rock bottom is. All of our thoughts are turned to grabbing onto some lifeline to help us climb out of there. Instead, when we realize we have hit rock bottom, we should start to dig the bottom out of that rock, so to speak.

If we continue to avert our eyes from our real situation, time will pass without our knowing. If we get medical treatment, it will keep us going to some extent. When we get swept away and end up wandering about all the time, that only puts off our awakening to our foolish nature.

## WORRIED? THINK!

When a person reaches their sixties, they cannot keep putting things off, saying they will do "it" later. The reason is, there is not that much time left anymore for them to do so. Medical treatment can only do so much for us, and after that there is nothing left for us to do other than look reality straight in the eye. However, that is the last thing we want to do, because it is unpleasant.

Some people would get angry if someone told them the truth about themselves. Then there are others who know but go on pretending not to know. Finally, there are those who are content to fool themselves. It is extremely difficult for people like these to arrive at an awakening to their foolish natures.

These people's difficulties are not unrelated to us. Everyone has this problem. The bookstores are full of personal advice books and self-help manuals. Live with a positive outlook, they write. If you think about unhappy things, you will fall into depression, so it is better not to think about them, they say. There are quite a few people who agree with this idea. Do not think sad things, shut them out of your mind!

It is typical of these books to repeat this advice to not think. When worried, you must think! When the actual nature of our worries is unclear to us, we must think. When young people are dissatisfied or uncertain and do not know what to do, they have trouble looking at the situation and giving serious thought to the matter. The nature of your problems may change over time to be greatly different from what it was long ago. Talking about what we don't like or thinking about what we don't like, is not what we like to do. So people leap to self-help manuals and "spiritual" books. It is not only the young who are this way; many adults are the same.

It might be because no one wants to talk about unpleasant things or even think about them.

In Buddhism, when we feel that we are immersed in the lovingkindness of the Dharma's liberation we can at last face those problems we do not like to talk about and those things about ourselves we do not want to hear. Those who do not know Amida Buddha's sincere (True and Real) compassion, however, want to run away whenever someone broaches such topics. Something must be done about this situation.

## To Go There is Easy and Yet No One is There

Once I attended a Buddhist service where the minister opened his Dharma talk by saying, "Dear friends, the fact that all of you have come here today is a matter of much significance. Attending a Buddhist talk would not be everyone's first choice for how to spend the day. It is thus a matter of significance that you have come with the intention to listen to this talk." I thought this was a great way to begin. It is indeed praiseworthy to note that the participants' connection to Buddhism had deepened to the point that they were ready to receive what the speaker had to say. It was an important point to praise.

One might ask if the only time that Jodo Shinshu is brought to our attention is at some unhappy or trying time in our lives. That is not the case. Just the fact that you come to listen to a sermon indicates that you have met with something in life that has led you here. Unless the conditions for awakening have matured, there is not much point to asking the listeners to take notice of what the minister has to say in the first place.

If it took someone who had led an exemplary life in this world, who vowed to go to the rescue of those in misery and impart them with the Dharma, it would not be possible for a person like myself to go to realize awakening. However, the heart of compassion is so broad that it embraces all sentient beings without any of the distinctions made by the human world.

It is my basic mission as a Buddhist to clarify the path by which Buddha's Sincerity (True and Real) comes to our rescue, and to clarify that there are living beings to be rescued.

In the case of someone who is seriously ill, however, mentally they are ready to throw themselves on the mercy of the powers that be and to be saved. So if one tells them, "There is no need to worry, just leave everything to Suchness," that is all that they need to hear for the message to get through.

However, for those who are not so desperate, such a message does not seem to work for them. The ordinary person is a creature of comfort, ready to embark on a journey without thinking, never giving a thought to the matter even up to the time he embarks. So it says in the *Larger Sutra of Immeasurable Life*, "To go there is easy and yet no one is there."

## Even the Funerals are Automated

Although we try to deal with everyday problems immediately, sometimes we confront situations that offer no easy solution. At those times the seams burst open and all the problems spill out. That is the nature of life.

We talked about graves before, so now let us look at funerals. Recently there has been an increase in so-called fast track funerals, where, once a person dies, their corpse is taken from the hospital to the crematorium where it is cremated right away. The End. It is all right if people call a minister in, but there are some who think, what is the point of calling a priest to chant a sutra and give a sermon, and so they decide not to do so. Such cases are on the rise.

Somewhere along the line, life has come to be an entirely clear-cut affair, with its events flowing downstream like a line of individualized components bumping up against one another. When you get sick you go to the hospital, if they cannot do anything for you then you die, your body is cremated, and you are just a pile of ashes. This is what you might call the assembly line of life.

It costs money, so we don't want to call a minister. Same goes for the funeral. This is not just a problem of economics. It touches on the growing sense of meaninglessness that we have been saddled with. This is the intrusion of what has been called nihilism into our lives.

When we talk about funerals in this way, it might sound like a spiel for the territorial rights of ministry. However, what I am really taking issue with is the infiltration of this way of divvying up everything in life into clear-cut little pieces.

After all, is life itself all that clear-cut?

When a small child dies, for instance, I doubt there is anyone who would say that such an event was a clear-cut one that we could have anticipated. At the same time, there seems to be a growing trend to avoid taking notice of death. This is possibly because death no longer connects us to a feeling of grief.

Is there no feeling of sadness that wells up from the depths of the heart when your parents or grandparents die? Death is an opportunity for us to experience the existence of something within us that we did not know existed. In other words, death puts us in touch with a part of our self that we normally are not aware of. It is our connection to death that makes us sit up and take notice of this aspect of ourselves.

Long ago, I met a doctor who became a minister just because of such a connection to death. When I asked him about it, he said he used to be a doctor at a coal mine. People there were dying on such a daily basis that he barely had time to take off his lab coat. He would end up sleeping on, and waking up on, his own examination table every day. He had seen so many people die from such a young age that he felt nothing when it came to thinking about the death of any living being. After all, it was just another biological event, he thought.

And then one day his dog died. Dogs do not live long compared to humans. While everyone knows that, the doctor was so grief-stricken over his dog he couldn't do anything. He could not believe how upset he was.

He was so surprised by what happened to him that it became an opportunity for him to notice something about himself. In the course of trying to understand his experience, he discovered the teachings of Jodo Shinshu, and later was ordained as a minister.

Something completely unexpected had welled up from inside the good doctor when his dog died. He understood this event leading to his awakening as a kind of reverse connection, when something that occurs out of order (such as the death of one's child) triggers a connection. Such reverse connections are trying experiences. It can open up an opportunity to think about death.

"Man is bound to die"—nothing's more certain, yet we refuse to think about it and keep trying to avoid it.

## What Starts at Death?

When a person is notified that they have only a few months left to live due to terminal disease, it is from the time they are notified that the mourning begins.

This is due in part to our aging society. It is not unusual to find people with parents in their nineties. This has given rise to "notified grief."

When the actual death takes place, there are cases where there is no grief left in the heart. People use up all of their grief in the period leading up to the actual passing.

There are also cases where the sense of bereavement is lost after a long period of nursing an elderly parent and taking them from one hospital to another. Then once the parent is gone, the feelings of sadness or loss have been so worn away that there is nothing left to feel. In that case, people have no qualms about skipping the funeral. Is this a kind of preparation for death on the part of the bereaved?

One might remember all the hardships the deceased has endured on our behalf, but no feeling of sadness comes up at parting. It is as if this winds up our preparatory seminar and the actual event of death does not signal the start of anything. Everything has been bundled up and finished before anything has begun.

As medical science advances and more people live longer lives, the opportunities to feel that life is short and gone before we know it, grow fewer. When the period of nursing and care is long, the heart grows weary, does it not? Advances in medicine are good, but by the same token it has ushered in the shallowing of our sense of death.

It might be a hard thing to hear, but originally, the long period before death was the time for a person to get his life in order. Something gets set right when a person has this time for himself. Once that person has died and those that held him dear have recovered from the experience, they might think about him again, remembering the dying period as a time their loved one had to compose himself for his final event.

There is a book by Shuichi Kato called *Shinran: One Aspect of the Thought Systems in the Thirteenth Century*. In it he describes the deep despair and suffering that pervaded the outlook of people of that age. This is history, completely forgotten with the long period of peace that ensued in the Edo period. When the world enjoys peace, our ability to see deeply rapidly disappears. Modern Japan is in an age of peace and prosperity, and death has grown superficial and distant to our everyday life. Now is an age when death has gone into hiding.

In a period like this, we must ask what needs to be done to make people realize that "Man is bound to die" and to awaken to the finitude of life.

CHAPTER 4

# SHINRAN'S WAY OF LIFE

*I know truly how grievous it is that I,*
*Gutoku Shinran, am sinking in an immense*
*ocean of desires and attachments.*
—*Kyogyoshinsho*

## A LIFE FILLED WITH TURBULENCE

What kind of life did Shinran Shonin, the founder of Jodo Shinshu, lead?

Shinran Shonin was born in Hino, south of Kyoto, in 1173, in the final years of the Heian period, more than eight hundred years ago. This was a period in Japanese history when the country underwent dramatic change, as it shifted from a long period of aristocratic rule to that of a *bushi,* or warrior class, government.

This was an era of political instability and internal struggle for Japan. Plagues spread throughout the land with natural disasters and famines striking one after another. Everyone lived in fear and uncertainty. Politically this was an age of extremes. It was during the violent struggle between the regent rulers of the Fujiwara clan and the cloistered emperors of the Imperial family that the new political force of the bushi rose to power.

Shinran Shonin saw the uncertainty of people in ordinary life firsthand. Worried and suffering himself, he lived a life full of tumultuous change.

Spending his youth focusing on monastic practice on Mount Hiei, he came to entertain doubts as to whether it was possible for

Buddhism to save all living beings. Finally, he decided to descend the mountain. Through the spiritual guidance of Honen Shonin (1133-1212), he was able to encounter the teaching of the exclusive practice of nembutsu. Shinran even married. However, due to court intrigue, he was exiled to Echigo (present day Niigata Prefecture). After about four years, Shinran Shonin's exile ended. He traveled to and settled in the Kanto area in eastern Japan and spread the Dharma (teachings).

Living a life full of worries and suffering just like an ordinary person, Shinran Shonin had the insight to return to his foolish self. In this chapter, we will focus on his life and discuss his teachings.

## SHOULD THE WINDS BLOW DURING THE NIGHT

Shinran Shonin is believed to have been born to a low-ranking aristocratic family descended from the Fujiwara clan. His family was famous for Confucian studies and waka poetry, and one of his uncles was a confidant to the former emperor Goshirakawa, who was a powerful figure of the time. There are virtually no historical materials relating to Shinran Shonin's childhood.

It is said that it was this uncle's plan to have Shinran Shonin ordained at the young age of nine and to enroll him in the Buddhist monastery on Mount Hiei. As to why he was ordained at such an early age, there are many theories, but none can be said to be definitive. Nine years old would make him the age of a present day fourth grade student. Whether or not a child of that young age could have any special thoughts regarding becoming a Buddhist monk, there is the following episode from his life that has come down to us.

It was when the cherry blossoms were in full bloom that young

Shinran Shonin was taken to a temple called Shoren-in to be ordained. It was evening when they arrived, and so it was decided to postpone the ceremony until the next day. In response to this suggestion, Shinran Shonin is said to have recited the following poem:

> *Ah, the heart that thinks to leave it till the morrow*
> *is like the fragile cherry blossoms hanging on the limb—*
> *Who knows whether a storm might visit during the night*
> *and scatter them to the winds?*

It could well be that if we put off seeing the cherry blossoms now in bloom, a storm will blow them away during the night. After all, this is the world of impermanence, and there is no guarantee of a tomorrow. This is what the poem means.

Whether or not this episode is historical fact is moot, but it does convey the sense of urgency that surrounded Shinran Shonin's Buddhist ordination and that those who held Shinran Shonin in adoration sought to express.

## Giving Up on Monastic Practice and Descending the Mountain

Shinran Shonin spent twenty years on Mount Hiei, from the time he entered the Enryakuji temple at the age of nine until the age of twenty-nine. The monastic life on Mount Hiei was a tense and demanding one. Shinran Shonin made great effort to meet these demands.

The actual Enryakuji monastery of the time was a place that prided itself on its very high standards for those wishing to study Buddhism in all its aspects. Its curriculum, like a modern university, offered a diverse program of study including Confucianism and waka poetry.

After twenty years of practice, Shinran Shonin, at the age of twenty-nine, descended Mount Hiei and placed himself under the tutelage of Honen Shonin. What change of heart took place in Shinran Shonin that made him give up the life of monastic practice and study he had so vigorously pursued?

While on Mount Hiei, Shinran Shonin pursued a life of extreme monastic practice. By such practice and upholding the precepts, which meant suppressing blind passions and seeking wisdom, he sought to become a Buddha. However, he came face to face with the reality that there are many who cannot pursue such practices and thus cannot be thereby liberated.

Of course, it was never the view of monastic Buddhism, which was called the Holy Path of self-power, to merely enlighten the self and not think of anyone else; that would be highly unsatisfactory. If I can mature spiritually to the point that I awaken to enlightenment, from that moment on I would hope to liberate those whom I meet. This Buddhist ideal, that if I am liberated, then I will work for the liberation of others, is to be aspired to. However, there is no telling when a particular monk will have a spiritual breakthrough and attain the realm of enlightenment. It is also possible that a person does not have the ability to arrive at that realm in the first place.

Is it possible for me to become enlightened? And is it possible for me to liberate others? These were the questions that Shinran Shonin encountered, I contend. When he looked at society at large and thought of the liberation of all living things, he must have felt, "This alone is not enough to deal with the problem." If the problem only involved himself, there would have been no necessity for him to give up monastic practice and descend the mountain.

It was when his narrow me, myself, and I, point of view

broadened its scope to include we, ourselves, and us, that he began to entertain grave doubts about continuing life as a monastic on Mount Hiei. This is what I would contend.

For his era, Shinran Shonin lived to the unusual age of ninety. The period of practice on Mount Hiei from nine to twenty-nine would not even amount to one third of his life. In those days, the average lifespan was quite short. A man in his thirties was considered to be late middle-aged.

It could be that Shinran Shonin thought he had fully lived his life when he reached the age of twenty-nine. From a modern perspective, it would correspond to age forty or fifty, when people have reached a point in their careers where they say, "This is enough." It was that kind of decision that Shinran Shonin had reached. The problem gnawed at him and deeply troubled him.

It is unclear what triggered this great change that overcame him. He was living in a world of uncertainty, the power struggle between the aristocracy and warrior class was continuing, and the land was beset by famine and other natural disasters. When it is hard to get something to eat and disease is rampant, this has an impact on people. When living day to day is so hard, this is not a time when you assume you will live to be ninety. He must have felt a sense of urgency, thinking, "It's now or never," when he made his decision to leave Mount Hiei.

## A Buddhism for Those of Us Who Live in the Age of Uncertainty.

Before his encounter with Honen Shonin, Shinran Shonin undertook a one-hundred day seclusion at Rokkakudo. This was a temple in Kyoto associated with Prince Shotoku, the founder of Japanese Buddhism, in the sixth and seventh centuries. Shinran

Shonin was no doubt overcome by delusion and unsure whether to remain on Mount Hiei or to seek out Honen Shonin. So he secluded himself at Rokkakudo for one hundred days.

It was during this time that Shinran Shonin had a dream. In that dream, Avalokitesvara, the Bodhisattva of Compassion, appeared to him. It was a sign he needed to seek out Honen Shonin.

As mentioned above, when Shinran Shonin considered the final outcome of his life of practice on Mount Hiei, he was forced to admit that it was not enough. It would not be correct to say that his encounter with Honen Shonin changed him, but rather he was already decided in his mind to go to Honen Shonin. He had grown so tired of his situation and he actively sought change. That likely triggered his dream of Prince Shotoku. It was the burning desire for change. This was another sign.

Well, then, what sort of instruction did Honen Shonin have for Shinran Shonin after he descended Mount Hiei?

Honen Shonin preached the doctrine of "exclusive nembutsu practice." Essentially, nembutsu is the sole practice that Amida Buddha has selected for our sake. Therefore, to chant the name *Namuamidabutsu* is all that anyone needs do to be liberated.

Up to this point, Buddhism focused on practices that would result in enabling one to become a Buddha. However, a question arises in our minds as to whether we have the ability to become Buddhas. It could be we do not. In other words, this was a path of monastic practice for someone who had to be extremely advanced in order to succeed.

When the majority of people are simple, ordinary people, though, what are they to do?

The exclusive practice of nembutsu opens the door to liberation for every living being. How appropriate this was for people living in the world of uncertainty! This was the teaching that Shinran

Shonin received when he met Honen Shonin. In fact, gathered around Honen Shonin were monks and laymen, aristocrats and samurai, as well as ordinary men and women.

## His Meeting With That Good Man

Shinran Shonin chanted *Namuamidabutsu* while on Mount Hiei. However, it was through his encounter with Honen Shonin that *Namuamidabutsu,* for the first time, took on the meaning of a path of liberation for all living beings. In short, the meaning of *Namuamidabutsu* underwent a revolution.

Late in life, when Shinran Shonin was compiling his teachings, he wrote a *wasan* verse in which he considered Honen Shonin to be a person who must have come from Suchness (True and Real).

A person with no worries who might meet Honen Shonin would probably say, "Oh, I see," in a perfunctory way and that would be the end of it. A person of greater depth would be able to appreciate the beauty of Honen Shonin's mind. In that sense, Shinran Shonin was the right person for this encounter.

Their relationship struck a fine balance between "I just realized something" and "You just made me realize something." In the *Tannisho*, it says: As for me, I simply accept and entrust myself to what my revered teacher told me, "Just say the nembutsu and be liberated." Nothing else is involved. (*A Record in Lament of Divergences*, second edition, p. 5) Such was the trust that Shinran Shonin placed on his meeting with that "good man," his revered teacher, Honen Shonin.

## What You Are Looking For and What You Find

These days when a person has problems they want resolved, they may go to a temple or church, or read religious books. However, whatever one is looking for in religion may or may not perfectly match one's expectations.

When they do not match, one kind of seeker will say that this religion is not for me. Another kind of seeker, though, will find something in the religion quite different from what they expected, and seeing the value of it, will say, that "This is wonderful!"

In some cases, an encounter with religion will turn out to be a meeting with something unexpectedly wonderful. In the case of Shinran Shonin, what he found did not fit his expectations. What he found in his encounter with Honen Shonin was, rather, something incomparably wonderful that far exceeded all of his expectations.

If seekers were the only ones to ever encounter Buddhism, this would mean that the vast majority of modern people would have no opportunity to discover it. The reason is, most people will first want to know why do I have to study Buddhism, and why do I have to let myself be transformed by its power? Even if you do not consciously seek liberation in Buddhism, as long as you have a connection to it, Buddhism, meaning the power of the Dharma, will bring you to realize something about yourself and you will be a different person because of it.

It sometimes happens that people are at their wits' end. They have a problem that they must resolve. When they misunderstand Buddhism, they will be disappointed in what the teachings have to offer. There is a real concern that people will look for a quick fix or self-help solution. Instead, it is better that we take our time and look deeply for a solution. Always looking for a quick fix to our problems is, after all, a kind of bonno, that often leads to our undoing.

While we are listening to the Dharma, new understandings will come about. We will have a chance to examine life experiences in the light of Buddhism; to experience them anew, and perhaps to understand them from a different perspective.

There are other times when Buddhist study may take a form that borders on amusement, and yet there still exists the opportunity to hear something about Buddhism that will strike a chord in us. A seed will be planted within us. That, too, is significant.

While all this is going on, something will happen, and a bud will emerge. It might be half in fun, but if you take the opportunity to be in touch with Buddhism and make a connection with it, this may lead to a sudden blossoming of insight.

The current situation with modern education is such that it will not allow any viewpoint other than a scientific one. Without our knowing it, we are being cast in the mold of the modern scientific self. As a result, it is very difficult for our sense of being a part of Suchness to develop. Our present education system offers little opportunity to come in contact with Buddhism, and so young people are growing up without knowledge of it. As a result, their ego consciousness becomes even stronger. If they could only let go of that ego they would be much better for it. People are so attached to their egos that they place it at their center of consciousness. They are unaware of the cause of their delusion and suffering.

That is why so many people are so confused when they come to a Buddhist church or temple. This is the result of never having examined or questioned values they have been immersed in. Until they can do this, they will never be released from the condition of being controlled by bonno.

## A Marriage in Line with the Teaching

One major event that resulted from Shinran Shonin's encounter with Honen Shonin was that he married. To have a monk marry openly was rare at that time.

For a Buddhist monk to publicly eat meat or take a wife was unthinkable by the monastic standards of the time. Why, then, did Shinran Shonin marry Eshinni?

It was Honen Shonin's teaching that whatever you must do to get through life is fine, as long as you do it saying the nembutsu. Shinran Shonin took these words to heart and lived them. What Shinran Shonin made real was a marriage that was consistent with Honen Shonin's teachings.

To understand the significance of Shinran Shonin's decision, it is necessary to first know something about marriage during the Kamakura era. Views regarding marriage in Shinran Shonin's time were different from what they are now. The institution of marriage as we now know it had yet to come into existence. For example, there was no justice of the peace where you went to register your marriage.

If we look at their family tree, it is clear that Shinran Shonin and Eshinni were husband and wife. In present day Japan, the concept of marriage is deeply influenced by the Christian concept of marriage as a religious contract. However, in the distant past, marriage had no religious significance.

It is believed that around that time the ratio of men to women of marriageable age was one to three. That was because boys had a greater chance of dying in infancy. So, it is not helpful to impose our present day views of marriage on the past.

On Mount Hiei, at the end of the Heian period, there were many monks who secretly kept a wife outside the monastery. Those monks also maintained the appearance of being celibate. In the case of Shinran Shonin, however, he made his marital status public. This was significant because it showed that he understood marriage to be consistent with Honen Shonin's teaching.

Married life became a topic for Buddhist discussion. When Shinran Shonin married, the light of the teaching was shining upon the problems of married life and family life. I think we can say marriage played a role in driving Shinran Shonin's deepening realization of the Dharma. If Shinran Shonin had kept his marriage secret then, it might never have becomes a topic for Buddhist discussion.

For Shinran Shonin, his marriage was blessed with his loving wife Eshinni and many children. However, late in life, he had the bitter experience of having to disown his own son. We can well imagine that the issues of family life, for better or worse, became an important element of Shinran Shonin's Buddhist teaching.

## Just Say the Nembutsu and Be Liberated

Jodo Shinshu is not a teaching that says do this, do that. Jodo Shinshu is based on the teaching of Honen Shonin that whatever you must do to get through life is fine, as along as you do it saying the nembutsu. Whatever each and every person does is fine, as long as they can say the nembutsu authentically—that is the standard.

When Honen Shonin and Shinran Shonin were ordained, Mount Hiei was a bastion of monastic Buddhism that, from the very outset, sought to shut out sensory stimulation. Located in a peaceful mountain setting at a good distance from any cities, it was the perfect place to seek, living a quiet life governed by precepts. It was a place where monastics could live cut off from worldly life.

In this setting, the monastics could not marry or eat meat. They entered a strict world of following precepts where one could not do this, one could not do that. Through the eyes of the practitioner who entered the world of the Holy Path, however, it was through severing the bonds of worldly life that one could become free.

When a man does not have a wife, it is not necessary to support a wife. When a man does not have children, it is not necessary to take care of them. When a man does not have to be concerned about his wife and children, he is free to come and go as he pleases. The path of the monastic is thus one that cuts off and liberates a person from all of the hardships and headaches of having a family.

In the case of Shinran Shonin, however, who married and had a family, this narrow viewpoint was replaced by one that sees life from the far broader perspective of all sentient beings, that is, the collective existence of all living beings. Honen Shonin is not saying that we will be free from hardships by doing whatever we do as long as we do it saying the nembutsu. Our freedom comes, rather, from saying the nembutsu while we embrace the realities of life as our own.

The decision to marry or not depends on you; it is pointless to look to the nembutsu for guidance. We can say that Honen Shonin never married, but that does not mean anything, or we can say that Shinran Shonin married, but that does not mean anything either. Whether we marry or not, either way is fine as long as we each take the way that is our own. Whatever you must do to get through life is fine, sums it up nicely. What is important is that you make the nembutsu the way of asking your living self what it is doing as a whole.

A person who marries should be concerned about the problems that they have as a person who has married. While those who do not, need not. Both should make the nembutsu the method of inquiring into the problems of life.

## It's All Right to Worry, Just Be Yourself

When people start a job, there are all kinds of social responsibilities they must bear. Having a family, however, is a social responsibility that is different from those.

Family relations hold an important place in our lives. We can see that Shinran Shonin regarded the family as important. We can also see from the fact that he had to disown his eldest son when he claimed unique spiritual authority that having a family must have been a major heartache for Shinran Shonin. This is reflected in a wasan verse that he composed late in life.

Shinran Shonin also had to be concerned about his relations with his disciples. This point we will discuss later.

As a member of Honen Shonin's following, Shinran Shonin had to train students who would continue his teaching. It may have made him happy to see his circle of nembutsu followers growing wider and wider. However, the nembutsu community was also a source of concerns.

It is not possible to run away from our problems. We are not free to not worry. While saying the nembutsu, we must do so thinking, here I am in this situation, and just as I am, like this, it is all right for me to worry. This, too, is a kind of freedom.

## Oppression Stirred Up By Court Intrigue

It is often said that Shinran Shonin spent a happy six years serving Honen Shonin in Kyoto. What brought all of this to an end was the oppression of "exclusive nembutsu practice" that was stirred up by court intrigue.

The year before it happened, while ex-emperor Gotoba was visiting a shrine in Kumano, some ladies from the court paid a call on Honen Shonin's disciples to listen to the teaching of exclusive nembutsu. This angered the ex-emperor, and led to the issuing of an imperial proclamation in 1207 banning the nembutsu. Several of Honen Shonin's disciples were beheaded. Honen Shonin and Shinran Shonin were exiled, Honen Shonin to Sanuki (present-day Kagawa Prefecture in Shikoku) and Shinran Shonin to Echigo (present-day Niigata Prefecture).

Shinran Shonin was thirty-five when the imperial proclamation declared that he was no longer a monk. In Echigo, he had to live a religious life completely isolated from Honen Shonin and his disciples. This was a terrible situation, yet one biography relates that he saw it as an opportunity to practice with the many ordinary people living in the outlying areas. This was perhaps the biggest turning point in Shinran Shonin's life.

Instead of becoming bitter and upset over his exile and letting this consume him, he instead found new meaning in this new life. I think this is an important point. Rather than expend his energy trying to change reality, he turned its content and meaning to his advantage.

Also at this time Shinran Shonin declared that, "I am now neither a monk nor one in worldly life. For this reason, I have taken Gutoku (stubble-haired) as my name." (*Kyogyoshinsho*, Postscript, *CWS. I,* p. 289)

As you can see, "I am neither monk nor layman," is what he was saying. Even if the religious authorities declared that he was no longer a monk, it was impossible for him as a person who had decided to walk the Buddha's way, saying the nembutsu, to return to ordinary layman's status. Shinran Shonin's "neither monk nor layman" statement thus depicted his real situation and he therefore went on to call himself Gutoku Shaku no Shinran (literally, Shinran, ignorant and stubble-haired).

The name Gutoku means a shaved head to which the hair has grown back to create a short stubble. This reflected the reality of being at an in-between status where one looks neither like a monk nor a layperson. With his exile serving as an impetus, Shinran Shonin gained considerable insight into himself as a foolish person drenched in desires. Yet these are the very kind of persons that Suchness (True and Real) has promised to liberate equally, provided we seek refuge in the Dharma.

## Onward to the Eastern Frontier

Five years later, Shinran Shonin was pardoned. Instead of returning to Kyoto, however, he crossed over the mountains to the east to Kanto. He chose to go to the eastern area as another region to spread the Dharma.

The eastern areas of that time in Japan are often portrayed as vast wilderness without cultivated land, but this was not always the case. The area known as Hitachi had fertile farmland. Also, the people of that area were familiar with the nembutsu and the *Lotus Sutra*, and believed in Kannon Bosatsu (also known as Avalokitesvara, The Bodhisattva of Compassion).

With an audience that was already familiar with Buddhist teachings, what could Shinran Shonin do to transmit the nembutsu teaching he had received from Honen Shonin? Shinran Shonin had no special technique, and we may surmise that it was Shinran Shonin's living both a religious and a family life that profoundly affected the people of the Kanto area. There are many stories that have been handed down about his meaningful relationships with people in the area.

For example, once there was a *yamabushi* (mountain ascetic) named Enni Bennen, who was unhappy with Shinran Shonin's ways of teaching and sharing the Dharma, and not only wanted to block them, but even had a plan to murder him. However, Bennen was so touched when Shinran Shonin talked with him at his cottage that he became one of Shinran Shonin's disciples. Bennen started saying the nembutsu, and went on to spread the Dharma also. Shinran Shonin was quite proud of his new disciple, whom he renamed Myohobo, and came to depend on him, it is said. The story of Bennen has been transmitted in that area even in modern times. In fact, the number of other individuals from the area who shared deep relationships with Shinran Shonin over the years must have been considerable.

Most of Shinran Shonin's new disciples were, in this way, bushi and farmers from the Kanto area. These new disciples transmitted the teaching to the people in other areas. As like-minded people who practiced together, communities of followers formed. Later an influential group of twenty-four key disciples formed.

The fact that Shinran Shonin headed to the Kanto area is said to be a conscious decision he made. It would have been natural for him to return to Kyoto, but at age forty, he decided to set out on a new path.

Informing this decision were the words of Honen Shonin, written in a letter at age sixty-two, that have come down to us, saying, "When everyone bands together, this will only lead to disputes. This is not good. Each of you should go out on your own individual paths." This is what some scholars think may have influenced his decision.

For those exclusive nembutsu practitioners who experienced oppression, gathering in one place would only make them a target for the authorities. If this happened, it would mean the teaching would not spread. Some scholars explain the reason for his decision to leave the Kanto area and return to Kyoto in this way. If these interpretations are true, the basic underlying reason for his decision was to spread the teaching to those whom he had yet to meet, who were living in lands he had yet to visit. We must not forget these positive reasons behind his decision.

## Life in Kyoto

Shinran Shonin is thought to have returned to Kyoto around his sixtieth year. From the time he returned to Kyoto from the Kanto area, until the time of his death at the age of ninety, is said to have been a period when he concentrated on his writings.

He may have thought, "I am past sixty now, and how many more good years I have left I cannot tell." When you reach this age, it is hard to make plans. Planning itself becomes difficult as we try to imagine the years ahead.

Shinran Shonin could not assume that he would live to be age ninety or imagine he would complete his *Kyogyoshinsho* or compose his seventy-five verse wasan collection. He simply took care of whatever project he had before him, one after another. During this process, his life extended itself, until he was finally able to leave us a large number of writings.

Zen master Dogen died at age fifty-four. If Shinran Shonin had died before age sixty, what would have happened to his

*Kyogyoshinsho?* He would not have left us a single verse before he died. All of the clear expressions of his understanding of the Dharma that we now have would have been lost.

After he returned to Kyoto, Shinran Shonin continued his work of spreading the teachings of the Buddha. This may be understood by reading some of his letters. We do know the several places where he changed residence and it is quite certain Shinran Shonin did not live in comfortable circumstances.

Shinran Shonin's letters tell us that he received financial support from his followers, and so it is likely his life was an impoverished one full of hardships. However, because he left numerous written documents, we know he was not so poor that he could not afford writing paper. At the time, neither paper nor ink were inexpensive commodities. His *Kyogyoshinsho* could only have been written due to the support of numerous others.

There are some scholars who say that, apart from the years when he was in exile, life in Kanto was in a bountiful farming area and so he must have enjoyed good economic circumstances. However, historical materials from this period are minimal.

We do know that the Kamakura Shogunate government lodged a complaint against Shinran Shonin's followers and disciples. This means that Shinran Shonin's followers in Kanto must have had some kind of organized community. If there were no organization, there would have been no point to pursuing legal action against them.

In his letters, there is acknowledgement of receipt of money. This means that his supporters had enough income that they could send some of it to him. If we think of a religious community of several thousands of people each making a small contribution, it could well be that they were able to provide him with the financial support he needed to go to Kyoto and concentrate on his writing projects.

Most of his main work, the *Kyogyoshinsho,* was written in a scholarly fashion as a doctrinal defense and reads like a dissertation. It was not the kind of material that would have been used in sermons.

However, in his letters, he often urged his followers to read works like *Yuishinsho* (*Essentials of Faith Alone)*, and others. That is, he was recommending that they read works written in *wabun* (everyday Japanese) and by contrast, works like the *Kyogyoshinsho* were written in *kanbun*, or classical Chinese. The *Kyogyoshinsho* is made up largely of quotations from Buddhist literature, in order to defend Honen Shonin's teachings. It is unclear how well the followers and disciples could have read and understood that work. We must, therefore, suppose that this was written as an academic work.

While one purpose of writing these works was to explain things, we must not overlook the fact that he also knew of the difficulty in communicating the teaching to others.

## Disowning a Son Late in Life

Shinran Shonin spent the final years of his life in Kyoto. To deal with situations that were cropping up in the Kanto area regarding Buddhist doctrine, he sent his eldest son Zenran as his emissary. However, that move did not work out as planned. There was friction between Zenran and the Kanto followers and disciples. This event has drawn the attention of numerous scholars, but there is no one theory that can claim to be historical fact. Some of Shinran Shonin's letters tell us that the Kanto community had fallen into confusion and that the Kamakura Shogunate government was showing signs of concern.

To get this situation under control, Shinran Shonin had to

make the painful decision to disown his son. Shinran Shonin was eighty-four at the time. It must have caused him deep suffering to take this step. It must have been all the more painful for someone who was a family man to have to confront this unavoidable situation.

This was not just a rift in the family. There was financial support coming from the Kanto community and it was through this support that he was able to pursue his writing projects—there was that aspect of the problem to consider. The Kanto members had amassed so much power, however, that areas of conflict were starting to develop among them. Once a community is formed, these difficult problems are bound to arise.

Through his writings, we can tell that Shinran Shonin strove to corroborate and deepen his understanding of the Dharma. To my mind, the exceedingly fine arguments he made in the *Kyogyoshinsho* and the numerous revisions he made to his wasans convey the difficulty of transmitting the teaching, or could it be I am reading between the lines?

On January 16, 1263 (the eleventh month, twenty-sixth day of Kocho 3 by the lunar calendar), Shinran Shonin died at the residence of his younger brother Jin'u. He had had a career that spanned eighty years. Shinran Shonin died during the famine of the Kocho period and so even up to the very end he lived out his life in a world of want and insecurity.

Shinran Shonin wrote in the *Kyogyoshinsho*, "I know truly how grievous it is that I, Gutoku Shinran, am sinking in an immense ocean of desires and attachments and am lost in vast mountains of fame and advantage, so that I rejoice not at all at entering the stage of the truly settled, and feel no happiness at coming nearer the realization of true enlightenment. How ugly it is! How wretched!" (*Kyogyoshinsho*, Chapter III, *CWS, I*, p. 125).

That is, "Though I join the numbers of those who are sure to be born, I do not feel the slightest joy; how ashamed I am of myself, knowing what I know of myself from living in this world of blind passions." Shinran Shonin can be said to be a person who knew the foolish self all too well.

## Chapter 5

# As Imperfect as We Are

*Carefully take measure of your own capability.*
— *Kyogyoshinsho*

### What Exactly Do We Mean By Foolishness?

Up to this point we have been talking about how difficult it is for people today to understand the concept of awakening to their foolish selves. It occurred to me that we might think of this difficulty in awakening to our foolish nature from a slightly different angle. We might see it as marking our point of entry to the Buddha Dharma, which is also said to be difficult to encounter.

When our usual problem-solving methods fail and we cannot get anywhere by thinking, "What should I do next?" or "This plan should work," it begins to dawn on us we are up against a problem that is impossible to solve. When our attempts to make headway fail, in the end, we are forced to submit to the truth about our self. And so at last we encounter the foolish nature of our self.

The aspect of foolishness in the foolish self points to our lack of wisdom. What then is true wisdom in Jodo Shinshu Buddhism?

In Rennyo Shonin's *Gobunsho*, or *Letters of Rennyo*, there is one chapter called 'The Eighty Thousand Dharma Teachings' which says, "Those who are not concerned about their after life are considered to be ignorant persons, even though they may be well-versed in eighty thousand Dharma teachings; those who have resolved the matter of the life to come are described as wise persons, even if they are illiterate laymen or laywomen." The wise and the foolish mark the two ends of the spectrum. This is how I understand this story.

Rennyo Shonin is saying that the person of true wisdom is the one who knows of the Eternal Now, while the foolish person does not. In his letter titled *The White Ashes* (*Hakkotsu sho*), Rennyo Shonin tells us we should all quickly take to heart the matter of the greatest importance, the Eternal Now. That is, the life before us is what is important. The person who knows of the Pure Land is a person of true wisdom. When you start to talk about the Pure Land, however, the modern person will beg your pardon and say, "That is what happens after death and has nothing to do with me, so I have not the slightest interest."

From a materialist and positivist point of view, death is the end; there is nothing after that. And so we have people who are extremely concerned about themselves and they are searching for themselves. They have a compulsive desire to find out who they are, thinking that it will be too late after they die. If they do not have the ability to unravel the problem of nihilism, however, there is little hope they will be able to deal with the onslaught of impermanence when it plows into them head-on.

Until we ask ourselves why it is that Rennyo Shonin called those who took the Eternal Now into their consciousness the wise and those who did not the foolish, we can never awaken to the foolish nature of our self.

I am inclined to think this could well be due to a sheer lack of opportunity. We live in a society that does not consider the Eternal Now, and so there are few opportunities for individuals to encounter it. How then are we to come across an opportunity to awaken to the foolish nature of our self?

## Returning to Our Naked Self

Now let us examine how the theme of awakening to the foolish self is treated by various scholars within Jodo Shinshu.

Yoshikazu Ishida (*b.* 1928), a professor at Ryukoku University, Kyoto, spoke on the theme of awakening to the foolish self. He pointed out that what Honen Shonin and Shinran Shonin meant by returning to the foolish self is not the same as being a foolish person. While these two phrases are only a little different in their original phrasing, there is a world of difference in their meaning.

In a research article Ishida indicated, "awakening to one's foolish self" means that one realizes the inherent limitations of his existence, recognizing it as an existential problem of his own as well as one that is universally valid, to be recognized in his relation to what is transcendent. This awakening takes place in the dimension of knowing, thus it is a fundamental problem *(Shinshu Kenkyu*, Vol. 47, p. 230).

Though Yoshikazu Ishida couched his argument in difficult philosophical terms, what he wanted to point out is the difference between a relative awakening and an absolute awakening. When a person who has not met with Suchness (as in the Vow of Amida Buddha) has an awakening, the awakening he has cannot be an awakening to the foolish nature of the self. This awakening is not to make a value judgment of whether one is foolish or not relative to someone else. Thus, Ishida is saying that awakening to the foolish nature of our self is a problem that takes place wholly within oneself. It forces one to inquire into the very ground of one's very existence.

Ryumyo Yamazaki (*b.* 1943), a professor at Musashino University, Tokyo, in a newspaper article titled, *Why Shinran Now? Returning to Our Ordinary Self, with a Spring in Our Step*

(December 18, 2007, *Tokyo Shinbun*, Evening Edition), tells the readers, "Shinran Shonin writes in a letter that Honen Shonin was fond of saying, '*Return to the ordinary foolish self–living without restrictions.*'" In other words, we must return to our true selves. Our degrees in education, the titles we have earned, the things we have achieved—we must detach our selves from the concerns about all of it. When we return to our ordinary selves, we give birth to an insight to the self in its simple beauty with all its foolishness intact. At that point we glean an insight into the self as interconnected with life in all its complexity. Here, too, Ryumyo Yamazaki is talking about returning to the ordinary foolish self and not the foolish self as a relative distinction, when for example, one says that such and such a person is an ignorant and foolish person who knows nothing.

Narumi Asai (*b.*1935), a professor at Ryukoku University, Kyoto, in a book titled *What We Can Learn from Shinshu* (Kyoto: Nagata Bunsho-do), wrote about returning to the foolish self, saying, "When we look back at all the things that we have, such as our position in society, all our worldly belongings, and even our family ties, none of it is the result of our efforts alone. Depending on the times and circumstances, it may well be that we will have to stand by and watch helplessly while all of this is lost. This is the way that we truly are, that one hears in nembutsu. The nembutsu guides us as we take our place as just another person living their life in the world. In nembutsu we never lose sight of this stark naked self of ours that is our starting point and point of return." Narumi Asai emphasizes "this way that we truly are," that is, the foolish selves that we are.

## All Because We Incur a Debt We Can Never Repay

There is a time in life where all the titles you have earned and all the things you have achieved are not able to help you. This is when we realize our mortality. This is also referred to as impermanence or "old age, sickness, and death," the final stage that we must all confront.

This is when our inner strength fails us, where nothing we have materially is of any use. When we become aware of this, that is when we start to turn to the foolish self.

We live in an age steeped in a human-centered way of life. We have to peel off all the layers of that life one by one. Through this process we get to the core of our existence where the true form of our self reveals itself. This is the point we must reach.

When we arrive at that point, we notice that the last thing we want to do is to change and to do something to make up for all the things we have done. When we finally admit to this real self, that this self is the last to reform, we feel like we have at last recognized reality. This happy outcome, though, is virtually impossible for modern people to achieve.

Modern people often have no feeling of guilt when they do nothing to make up for doing something bad; in fact, the thought to do so never occurs to them in the first place. They have no awareness of what they have done. When the wall of our awareless state crumbles, though, the world suddenly appears to us to be a totally different place. We look back and say, "Ah, now I see that I was not aware that I was like that." A broad new vista opens up to us.

The motto the previous Monshu was fond of recognizes the need for such awareness. It was made up simply of, "We partake of this meal" and "Thank you," two phrases that could be used to express gratitude at mealtime. As I pointed out before, there is no way we can pay for the life we consume. We cannot compensate the fish for its life. When we take note of that fact, we become free of our bonds to this human-centered world in which we are enmeshed. The word "life" takes on vast new meaning as we see ourselves as part of all sentient beings. Every time we partake of a meal, there is no way we can pay back the debt we owe to the plants and animals for the life we receive from them.

Recently, there was a program to raise pigs and chickens in the elementary schools, and once they were raised, to process them into food to be eaten by the students. This brought a powerful reaction by those who were opposed to such an educational program. However, unless people understand what eating truly entails, they cannot see the complete nature of human beings who incur a debt to other living beings that can never be repaid.

The farming and fishing communities of Japan have for centuries conducted memorial services for the crops and fish they have harvested. They honor the lives of the food they eat, and they have a feeling that they are sorry they have to do this to survive. The ceremony expresses the feelings of regret of the farmers and fishermen that they have to consume, even so. In contrast with the attitude that we can settle our karmic debt with cash, this old memorial service custom can be said to have a warm feeling towards life.

## Why There Are All Life Form Services in Jodo Shinshu

Human beings are creatures who have accumulated a tremendous debt to life that they can never repay. When we recognize this in our selves and try to atone for the debt, we find that, whatever actions we might take, there is nothing that can clear this debt. Even if we were to perform this memorial service, there would be nothing that can be saved.

If there were a life we hoped to rescue but could not, this means we had to draw a line somewhere that resulted in life being cut short. When a life must be lost because we had to draw the line, that means we cannot expect to save every life as we had hoped, nor will our actions to do so ever achieve that desired result.

Such customs as the memorial service for plants or animals are expressions of the painful awareness that people have. Such customs are not to be laughed at or ridiculed; rather, we should feel the pain people must feel. It is important to understand how people feel and why they feel compelled to perform such a memorial ceremony for, while they have managed to stay alive, they feel they must do something for the sake of the living beings that did not.

When Shinran Shonin first arrived in the Kanto area, he was witness to a terrible famine and began chanting the three Pure Land Sutras a thousand times. He could not be present in that situation and do nothing, yet there was nothing he could do. There was nothing he could do, and so he thought he should chant these sutras. In the midst of his effort, he realized it was all in vain and he stopped.

It is not an easy matter to look yourself straight in the eye and admit that what you are doing makes not the slightest difference in the world. Shinran Shonin had to undergo numerous painful experiences to arrive at the stage he did.

Shinran Shonin looked human limitations directly in the eye. He had to share with people that there was another power that is bestowed upon us.

The recognition of humanity as those whose wishes never

come true is also expressed in the Jodo Shinshu teaching itself. In the *Tannisho* are the words, "In our present life, no matter how much our hearts may go out to someone we love, it is impossible to rescue them as we wish, and so such compassion as we hope to achieve never gets fully realized. Note well, though, that simply by saying the nembutsu alone, this is the great compassionate mind that brings all our hopes around full circle" (chapter 4).

To paraphrase, as long as we are living in this world, no matter how sorry we may feel for someone suffering or think it too bad they are suffering so, there are many cases where it is impossible for us to go to their rescue, as much as we wish we could. Such compassion as we feel, then, cannot be perfect. And so it is only in saying the nembutsu that we find the thoroughly-perfected heart of Great Compassion.

Shinran Shonin knew that a human is being born with limitations. He told those who listened, however, that there was a world where they could feel Suchness at work as it embraced humans in their suffering and strove to support them in their limited sphere.

## Those Who Do Not See the Eternal Now as Our Ultimate Concern

Fortune telling and lucky charms are forms of superstition and folk belief. Even a perfectly reasonable person may encounter a problem that is beyond their abilities and may turn to superstition or magic to try to make their wishes come true. In the end, though, they find out that their wishes have not been fulfilled.

If fortune telling and lucky charms have any meaning at all, it is that they make us realize how weak we are. In today's world, this weakness has been capitalized on and made into a profitable industry. People are cleverly rounded up and thoroughly exploited, and then dismissed, when of no further use.

There is a point where religion breaks through such folk belief. In Jodo Shinshu we uncover a view of humanity with critical depictions of the self: as those whose wish for eternal life that is not granted, as those in need of awakening to the foolish self, as those whose status is that of karmic evil.

In our contemporary world, it has become quite impossible to notice these things about our self. It used to be that to get food on the table, the fish that was caught was still flopping around. Someone had to kill it so it could be filleted and served.

Today, when you go to the supermarket, you only find pieces of fish. For beef, you see only packaged products, nothing else. The fish and beef we purchase at the market seem to have no real connection to living animals. This is why we do not have a real sense of living life, and at the same time we have no real sense of death and dying.

Why is it that we have no real sense of life or death?

This is because, in the modern world in which we live, our role is that of the consumer. We touched on this point at the very outset.

Shinran Shonin commented on this subject, saying, "Such peddlers, hunters, and others are none other than we, who are like stones and tiles and pebbles" (*Yuishinsho mon'i*). The current concept of ourselves as consumers blocks the reality of what we are.

Philosopher Tatsuru Uchida (*b.* 1950) coined the phrase "the consumer mind." It does not matter if one is a child or an adult, as long as one pays, the shopkeeper will treat everyone equally as customers. No one cares whether you are old or young, man or woman—a person who has a thousand dollars to spend is treated as a customer spending a thousand dollars.

What kind of effect has this consumer mentality had on child development? They do not need to know or care or have any interest in where an item was made or where it came from. As long as they have cash, they become the consumers. When this happens, the main problem of life becomes all the more difficult to see. The one great matter of life starts to disappear from view.

## Modern Man as Lacking in True Wisdom

As far as the consumer is conditioned to believe, the cheaper a product is, the better, but that is such a narrow way of thinking. At one time, the phrase, "a free-fall in prices" was popular. It is unclear to me what exactly was behind this phenomenon. So-called economists seemed to think it best to leave the free market economy to itself.

The difference in prices was not only a problem in Japan. There was a difference in the wages between Japan and other countries. Japan's high wages put Japanese-produced goods at a competitive disadvantage as far as price was concerned, and so corporations started to shift production to foreign countries. However, merely to be enthralled with the promise of savings brought about by the free-fall in prices is to fail to consider the problem of the hiring of workers.

A society cannot function if it is built on economic principles alone. In recent years, the deregulation of the economy has accelerated part-time employment of workers such that they now make up more than thirty percent of the work force. In Japan, the work place has started to crumble. When the world economic crisis hit, the practice of corporations reducing their work force and refusing to hire new employees jeopardized the bonds that hold Japanese society together.

By over-emphasizing consumption, economists have chosen to ignore that we are also producers of what we consume. What in the world do we have in mind when we put ourselves in such a compromising position? This is not a wise course of action and indeed can only be called downright foolish. It is the unawakened state of those who have yet to awaken to the foolish nature of the self.

If the wish for ever lower prices were to come true, there would be no way to avoid the downward spiral of workers' wages. Japan seems to be headed toward a major contradiction by following this marketing principle, and it remains to be seen how it will affect the ordinary citizen. All the while the investment funds, large banks and corporations are busily reaping profits.

Poorer countries that have nothing to export can and will export their labor force. The global economy allows cheap labor to be sent overseas. It is as if people are being bought and sold.

## The Illusion of a Global Economy

There are those who sing the praises of the global economy. The entire world will enjoy prosperity as the economic level is raised and so this bodes well for our future, it is said. At present, however, there are billions of people living in advanced countries. There are seven billion people in the entire world. If the entire population of the earth underwent economic growth, would it be possible for the planet to sustain such an economy?

It is unlikely that food supplies, natural resources, and energy resources will last. When the resources are exhausted, the rich countries will need to lower their standards of living from what they had enjoyed. When we look at the actions of the world leaders of the global economy, however, it is unlikely that they will willingly agree to follow such a course.

Global industries turn a profit when there is a difference between the haves and have-nots in terms of capital, resources, and so on. This is especially true of the financial market.

If everything were equal, the sweet spot for big business in the economy would disappear. Companies would start to go out of business. If currencies were standardized, the currency exchange would not be needed and those who make a living off of the difference in rates would be out of a job. So we must ask ourselves if this is really what we want. Even if this were possible, it probably would have to take place on a scale spanning centuries. In the meantime, how many generations of people would have to sacrifice their lifetimes to the cause?

Can those people who promote a global economy based on the principle of competition be serious in their stated desire for prosperity for all humankind?

In the oil-rich Arab countries, foreign laborers are employed, and there are many people there who live like kings. If everyone were to live an affluent life, however, there would be no one who would go to these countries to work as maids and servants.

In Japan, part-time workers make up one-third of the entire work force. Those who call for anti-regulatory measures are not seeking to provide a better life for all. Their idea is that as long as labor costs are low, that is all that matters. We must ask what kind of standards they are applying for our life in society, when their view seems narrow in the extreme.

Their narrow view is not only in terms of the economy. They are also narrowly human-centered and self-centric, and have forgotten the broader view that takes all living things into consideration. This is the serious problem that modern man confronts.

## A Doctor Is Not Almighty

The same thing has happened to the medical profession. Now there is a right to deny medical treatment.

An emergency room doctor told me about this right. He told me not to call it the right to deny medical treatment, but rather the inability to provide medical services. Since there have been big cuts to the national health services budget, the funds available for operating costs for emergency medical services have also been cut. There are insufficient funds to employ enough medical personnel, and no one is willing to do anything. These days, also, any small medical error can result in a lawsuit. This being the case, there may be no way to get around the right to deny medical treatment.

From the patients' point of view, they take it for granted they will receive adequate medical treatment even in the emergency room. They go there thinking that of course the doctors will help them, but to put it rather bluntly, that is only a sweet dream. We are only deluding ourselves to feed our strong desire to live.

There is, of course, a world of difference between emergency medical care that saves lives and that which does not. It is just as sure that we have lost sight of the fact that humans are born to die.

Since the doctor is not infallible, it is not possible for the finest medical care to be provided at all times. This, however, is what the patient expects. Here, too, the patient has lost sight of the reality of the matter of the life hereafter.

Where do we draw the line between there is hope for this patient, but there is no hope for that one? For once in our life we need to awaken to our ignorant self and admit the fact that no one knows what we should do.

Patients and their families have all become consumers of the medical profession. Consumerism is a word that people are not fond of. It is a word that expresses a direct link to our desires. Alas, the desires of consumerism expand with no end in sight!

## A Decision Which is Not Thorough

There is an aspect to our desires and blind passions that leaves us thirsting and craving for more. It is because they always leave us thirsting and can never be satisfied that they are called blind desires. Unless we become aware of the reality of these desires and blind passions, there is no way for us to rein them in.

When a disaster occurs and emergency medical teams arrive on the scene, the first thing they must do is known as a triage, sorting out the patients for available treatment. The treatable ones have top priority. There are no words to console those whose loved ones were victims of disasters, but there are always those who are beyond medical care. Finally, there are those who are only slightly injured who can be looked after later. For the medical teams to do their job, these patients have to be placed in some kind of order.

In 2005, when the Fukuchiyama train disaster occurred, the accident scene was complete pandemonium. The medical teams handled triage by placing colored tags on the victims. The black tag announced to the injured, "We are sorry, but it is too late for you, you are beyond medical care." Though our hearts go out to these victims, we must also remember the psychological suffering this must have caused to those who had to make those decisions. It is hard on a person of conscience to have to decide who will live and who will die. However, someone has to make this decision in order for the emergency rescue operation to go on, effectively.

There are few hard and fast criteria for this decision making process. It is just an imperfect decision that must be made.

There are the injured people waiting in line from some time, and there are the new arrivals who join them. Everyone knows the ones needing life saving care take priority, but after that happens, people will say, "Wait, I am in a lot of pain, so why are they taking care of that guy first?" It makes you wonder if you will last long enough to get treated.

In emergency medical care, when people's lives are at stake, it often happens that the medical staff has to draw the line somewhere.

From humanity's beginning we have been living a life that embraces that contradiction. Whatever the situation might be, there is no way we can possibly understand it in its entirety. That is, we must awaken to our limitations. This is what Shinran Shonin means by returning to the foolish nature of our self.

## Carefully Gauge Your Own Abilities

Shinran Shonin has these words of admonition to share, "You people who make up the priests and laymen of this defiled world, you would do well to carefully gauge your own abilities. Make note of this point" (*Kyogyoshinsho VI-1:14*).

Shinran Shonin here refers to our ability to realize and become enlightened. With these words he questioned our ability to leave behind the realm of *samsara* by our powers alone. In short, it is a critical comment concerning whether man has the capability to enlighten himself through his own ability.

It is evident that man is born lacking the ability to attain enlightenment through self-power. Humans live an existence that can neither compensate nor reform, and do not even have the capacity to bear these matters in mind.

Here we are not talking about the goods bought by the consumer. This is a question of the quality of life that each of us, as a consumer of life, is living. It is important that we let this point sink in.

When we give it some thought, we are pressed to admit that the individual who can neither compensate nor reform and who does not even have the capacity to bear these matters in mind, is none other than ourselves. It becomes clear to us, then, that for us to live minus these rather significant shortcomings is simply not an option.

When we take this into consideration, for the first time we are able to inquire as to just who is the foolish person? To my mind what Shinran Shonin meant by the foolish person is indicated by the following words, "The Buddha's Sincerity (True and Real) does not take up each of my deeds and evaluate whether it is good or bad. According to the teachings, rather, I am being accepted in my entirety."

In the secular world, a person is judged on the basis of certain acts regarded to be wrong. Indeed there are those who have committed terrible crimes, and there are some acts that are thought to put us beyond redemption. However, if we start to evaluate every deed people do, we will spend our whole life absorbed in judging someone else's life. If we start to compare ourselves with our peers, it would turn out that I am worse than that person but better than this person. Our judgments would slide up and down a relative scale of good and bad.

Shinran Shonin taught that it is clear that each and every one of our acts is significant. At the same time, it is not a question of whether each and every act is good or bad. When there are some things we simply cannot do anything about, the question is whether the concerns the whole human race burdens themselves with are ultimately worth considering.

As the *Tannisho* would suggest, the problem of good and evil is not a question solely of free will.

## YOUR ACTIONS GOOD AND BAD ARE YOUR KARMIC CONSTITUTION

Since the Dharma comes to the rescue of the karmically-compromised person, there is no need to fear committing wicked acts out of an overweening pride over the Vow—is this kind of thinking not a problem? Shinran Shonin explained it is not whether you willed your actions to be good or bad; rather, it is the working of your karma that prompts you to act. Even though all people are promised liberation, it doesn't mean that we are free to act any way we please, irregardless of right and wrong (*Tannisho* 13, *CWS,* p. 670). When we realize our karma is behind even a wrong as "tiny as a speck of dust on the strand of wool," for the first time we begin to realize what the awakening of a foolish person truly means.

In the *Tannisho*, the following famous exchange between Shinran Shonin and his disciple Yuien is given below. This is a modern version of the account. It is rather long.

The Shonin once asked me, "Yuien-bo, do you believe what I say?" "Yes, I believe what you say," I answered.

"Then you will not turn your back to whatever I say?" he asked me once again, and I affirmed that I would most respectfully not do so.

Once I had said this, he said to me, "First, will you not go out to kill a thousand people for me. If you do this, your birth in the

Pure Land will most definitely be assured."

At that point, I said, "Although that is what you, the Shonin, are asking me to do, someone like me cannot find it in himself to kill even a single person."

He then asked, "Well, then, why did you say you would not turn your back to whatever I say?"

He went on to say, "There is a point to be learned from this. If everything worked out the way we wished, the moment that I said, for the sake of birth in the Pure Land you must kill a thousand people, it should have been possible for you to go out and kill. However, since you do not have the karmic link to kill at will, it ends up that you cannot kill even a single person. It is not because your heart is good that you do not kill. Again, it might be you do not intend to kill anyone and will end up killing a hundred or a thousand people."

In today's world, a person who is ordinarily good in everyday life, may take part in war where he is forced to kill others. No one will hold him accountable for killing people; he is just doing the work of war. On the contrary, he might even be praised for his actions. In order to defend one's country, men will kill others given the rationale to do so. There are times when a man will do so with relish, and there are times when he will do so all the while hating what he does. It is not out of our free will that we act; rather, we are moving in the flow of something greater than ourselves.

The dimension in which Shinran Shonin responds to the problem of good and evil is not whether we do good or evil out of our free will. It is a question of what lies at the basis of our existence as human beings.

It is on this basis that we can say for the first time, "Even a good person attains birth in the Pure Land—so it goes without saying that an evil person will." Shinran Shonin also understood that, in order for men to live, we have to take the lives of other living things, otherwise there would be nothing for us to eat. Human life, as such, is an existence that embraces a fundamentally evil karmic nature. All living things in this world have this "karma" to bear.

## The Great Power We Cannot Do Anything About

By and large all a mother or father hopes for is that their children grow up to become mature, responsible adults. Do this, do that, they tell them, by way of disciplining them. Though they might be doing this out of parental concern, what often happens is they end up being too pushy toward their children.

These days we cannot read the newspaper without coming across distressing cases of abuse involving parent and child. I would suspect there are many cases in which a parent does not start out with the intention to abuse their child. Rather, it was their intention to discipline their children to be good that instead led to their abuse of the child. While we, of course, cannot condone rude behavior on the part of the child, the so-called good intentions of the parent can sometimes get out of hand.

Here we must gain an awareness of the great power that moves us beyond our considerations of good or bad.

In the *Tannisho* this great power that we can do nothing about is called our karma. In a word, it is our karmic condition in which we live.

The problem is that the word karma leads to misunderstanding. People who hear that it is a great power we can do nothing about will jump to the conclusion that it means, when we were under its sway, that we did not know any better at the time. This is not what it means.

In the last world war, the Japanese government made up slogans like "The Great East Asian Co-Prosperity Sphere," which spoke of freeing Asia from the Western colonial powers. This was one of many stories that the Japanese people were told. Stories have fascinated people in every age and if these stories have the power to move people during formative times, this will decide the direction of future events. And the consequence is always laid on the shoulders of each and every individual who participates in that chapter of history.

In other words, the result manifests itself as the suffering of the people. What can religion do for these people, is a question that religious leaders must constantly keep in mind.

Religion can make us aware of our self being moved within the current of the times. Also, there are times when we have no choice but to bear the brunt of responsibility for what has come to pass. I believe that religion exists to help us come to terms with what we have done.

Another wartime slogan was "Free the colonies." It had a ring of truth to it as far as words go. The reality of it, however, was far different. Those who thought it a splendid idea were all for it. However, once the dust settled and we saw the outcome, there were of course some disappointing features in the real situation. Are we to resign ourselves to them, or should we deny them and strongly insist the situation is perfect in every respect? The position that can accept the past as such has the potential to change the future. And so it is good if religion's view of man can give us this sense of direction in life.

We can try to evade our responsibility by saying, "We did not know better at the time," or "At the time we thought it was the right thing to do." It is possible to justify ourselves saying, what we did was wrong, but we were right in principle. We hear ourselves saying this kind of thing all the time, every day. However, this letting ourselves off the hook is denied by Buddhism.

Even if you did not know any better at the time, if what you did was wrong, you have to admit it, by saying, "I was wrong" and "I made a mistake." That one point has the power to change the past and the future at the same time. You may attempt to escape from your past into the future, but actually you cannot run away. Religion will give you the power to accept the past and future without having to live a lie.

## You Are Saved Just As You Are

Religions generally talk about salvation. One may think all forms of salvation are the same, however, they are not. The words might seem the same, but they often mean completely different things.

When we speak of liberation, it is necessary for it to have both a side affirming our self and a side denying our self. One part of liberation cannot allow our self to excuse itself by saying, "We did not know any better at the time." Another part of liberation, while not forgiving our self, sees that we are a tad foolish and so it accepts us so that we can come into a way to live in the future.

In my younger days, whenever I attended a sermon, I would often hear the words, "You are saved just as you are." It was hard to understand the expression and it left me confused as to what it meant. As far as the doctrine goes, it is in fact the case that Buddha's Sincerity (True and Real) saves us just as we are. What I felt uncomfortable with was the "just as we are" part. If that was so, that would mean there would be no need for self-reflection on our part.

For people living in this modern age, these words are rather dangerous. Recently we often hear words such as, "You will be saved just as you are, you are fine just as you are, you are OK just like that." This is the pitch of the "spiritual" movement and secular psychology that we touched on earlier.

If we just take the words at face value, it sounds much like liberation, "You are all right just as you are." In fact they are different.

Buddha's Sincerity (True and Real) saves us because we cannot do it ourselves. On our part, if we pretend that we are fine just like this, then there is no need for liberation. The reason that it must save us is because we would be lost if left to our own devices. It cannot leave someone like myself on my own. Buddha's Sincerity (True and Real) is extremely concerned about us.

When people are finding it hard to get out of the suffering they are caught up in, when they are laden with bad karma and all their efforts to save themselves by religious practices and good deeds are coming up short, they are in no condition to be left by themselves. For that reason Buddha's Sincerity (True and Real) is said to save us just as we are. This does not mean an absolute affirmation of who we are. Here we need to adjust our understanding.

To be remorseful is to feel ashamed of ourselves. It is important that we realize that we stand in need of liberation. When we stand on that plane of understanding, we become aware of the fact that Buddha's Sincerity (True and Real) itself has saved us. Then we are able to live in this moment of facing the future. Thus it is through our action of remorse that joy opens up to us.

## Narrowly Closed Up Within Myself

The psychiatrist Dr. Rika Kayama wrote that spiritual healing does not take into account the people around them. She points out that the difference between spiritual healing and religion is whether they are aware of others.

It is likely today's young people sense that other people are a source of irritation and trouble and so minimize face to face contact with them. That is why spiritual healing has such a strong appeal. It is because spiritual healing focuses on the self and does not take others into consideration. When this point is brought to our attention and we look around us, we notice that the things that are so popular with young people are invariably those that put the emphasis on the self. These are electronic devices like the cell phone or iPod that I can enjoy all by myself. In an extremely self-centered way, I am then closed off from the world and I am the only one there is.

People think that even their neighbors are irksome. Why is the life network, that we count on, breaking down? Even though the entire network of all sentient beings awaits us, we are not willing to open our hearts to it.

What may be causing the lack of connection is the absence of experiences where we do things together with others, filled with laughter or tears. When we do something meaningful with others, our relationships open up. When we do not, our feeling of isolation deepens. For some people the whole world seems to exist within their smart phone or computer. Such a person is not in an enviable situation.

We do not wish to remain trapped within our loneliness, and so we yearn for healing. Though we look for things to substitute for our suffering and sadness, we are fearful of looking loneliness straight in the eye. When a person has it in mind that society has failed them, in the end he becomes his own victim.

## Taking the Message of the Larger Sutra to Heart

What do we have to do to get out of this spiral?

When it comes to making friends, we need the support of someone we can trust. In order to establish this kind of relationship with others, I think it is important to keep in mind the heart of Buddha's Sincerity (True and Real). However, when it is put this way, many people are turned off by it, saying that is too preachy.

Here first it is necessary to understand the connection between human relationships and religion.

In human relationships, the words "someone you can trust" are understood to mean friends you get along with, who accept you as one of them when you go for a night out on the town. However, friends you think you can trust, in order to maintain good relationships, often are only putting on a good face. As a result, they sometimes will turn against you because of a misunderstanding over some small thing not really worth the trouble.

As we need to deepen our understanding of ourselves, the possibility opens up of a broader connection between ourselves and others. Earlier, we discussed why it was necessary for us to become aware of ourselves as being badly in need of liberation. If we have this understanding, then why is it that "This person cannot be left to save himself?" The reason is that there is nothing that is true or absolute about ourselves.

When we keep this in mind, it means we are aware of the vast and deep mind of compassion that accepts everything about us, that together with us feels the sadness we feel and walks along with us. Both you and I are supported by the same mind of compassion. This is what I want you to be aware of.

However, what words are suitable to convey this message to

the modern world? There is no easy answer.

There is a short sutra chant called the *Sanbutsu ge*, or Verses in Praise of the Buddha. It is chanted together by our followers during the service. One passage of it reads:

*Go sei toku butsu*
*fu gyo shi gan*
*issai ku ku*
*i sa dai an*

A translation of the text reads:

*I resolve that, when I become a Buddha,*
*I will fulfill this vow in every possible way,*
*And to all beings who live in fear*
*I will give great peace.*
–*The Three Pure Land Sutras, Volume I*

People often relate that they understand the sutra for the first time when they read the modern versions.

Even though Jodo Shinshu followers are used to chanting the sutras, sometimes I wonder. Even though they are familiar with the words, how do these words connect with them? It is rather difficult to reach the point where those words resonate in one's heart. Let me ask you, everyone, when the sutra says, "I resolve that, when I become a Buddha, I will fulfill this vow in every possible way, and to all beings who live in fear I will give great peace," to whom do you think these words are being addressed?

Also, traditionally, during the annual Shinran Shonin Memorial Service held in January each year, there is a passage quoted from *The Sutra of Immeasurable Life* that says, "I can remove the roots of suffering and affliction in birth-and-death," that is, the source of everyone's delusions and suffering will be eliminated. What does this root of suffering in birth-and-death refer to? The answer is not as simple as getting the correct answer on a test. Given time, the sutra will reveal to you an answer, provided that you yourself become the person who asks this question.

The words of the sutra must be planted in the heart of each person. It is not just a matter of understanding them, but planting the words in the heart that is important, is it not?

## What is Suffering?

The phrase, "The root of all suffering in birth-and-death will be pulled out," means that the root of suffering will be removed. However, what exactly do we mean by suffering?

Suffering, in samsara, is the extreme suffering that all people have to endure.

When translated from the Sanskrit, the word "suffering" means that things do not turn out as we expect.

Whoever we might be, since we are bound to grow old, become sick, and die, things do not turn out as we expect. We suffer when things do not turn out as we want, and suffering is born when we try to make them turn out as we expect.

When man wants things to turn out a certain way, that person's existence, as such, becomes filled with suffering. However, in the midst of suffering, human beings do not see it that way. Remorse, to be ashamed of oneself, to sense the pain, to look back and reflect on oneself is something people cannot do. When a person operates in a human-centered way, he is blind to the reason for his suffering.

Suffering is born when things do not go the way we expect. However, if everything went the way we expected, what a horrific situation we would be in. The world itself might fall apart.

Some time ago, when the Iraq war started, it was said the situation was not going the way we had hoped and expected. It made me wonder what kind of world it might have been if President George Bush and Saddam Hussein had gotten the world they expected.

This does not go just for political figures, but for ourselves as individuals as well: to hope that everything goes as we wish and expect is a dangerous thing.

## When Family Members Turn On Each Other

We hear news of terrible violent crimes taking place in society on almost a daily basis. As mentioned earlier, statistically speaking, the number of cases of violent crimes, such as murder, is actually decreasing. What is surprising, though, is that about half the murders in recent years are among family members. Family members are killing one another. What should be the safest place for us turns out to be the most dangerous for family and relatives to come together, and this is a worrisome situation.

If a person becomes irritable when things do not go as they expect, it is natural that a person might vent anger on them, because family members are felt to be safer targets. As the aggression grows in a person's heart, he will lash out at those nearest. This behavior may not be limited to family members. The aggressor wants others to see him as occupying a kind of privileged position. If we had to recognize their dominance and had to do whatever they wished, the world would indeed be a rather hopeless place.

The world of the internet is thought to be vast, but however extensive its information space, all we are seeing of it is what is on the screen in front of us, and so what we are seeing of human life is becoming extremely narrow. That is why bullying and badmouthing have become so prevalent and aggressive on the internet. Manners and refinement have no place there. In that narrow space, it is inevitable that the kind of person we find is one who has lost sight of the nature of human life.

The world of the internet and the smart phone is increasingly one in which, if there is something we do not wish to see, we simply do not look at it.

Internet users adopt the attitude that what they do not see does not exist in this world. This gives birth to oversized egos and people who seek to control others, thinking they are all powerful. The effects of this on immature children, who have no immunity to this kind of thinking, is worrisome. Even without the internet, they are already growing up in a human-centered world.

No matter how much the internet promises to make all our dreams come true, real society cannot be built upon that. Things do not always work out as planned for us, and that is the way life is. When that happens, our fond dreams may suddenly collapse in despair.

## Be Conscious of Suffering

So that this does not happen to you, it is important to be conscious of suffering.

One of the basic Buddhist teachings is known as the Four Noble Truths, that is, the truth of suffering, the truth of our gathering it to ourselves, the truth of its possible extinction, and the truth of the path leading to its extinction.

This might be a difficult teaching to understand, but let us give it a try since it is a basic Buddhist teaching. First, let us begin with the truth of suffering. This points out the truth that this world is full of suffering, and that all living things are bound to suffer in order to live. To put it in simple terms, life is a bumpy road.

When someone stumbles on the road of life, people think it odd. That is, they assume that the way through life should be smooth and without suffering. That assumption is mistaken.

Next, the formation and arising of suffering, the cause of suffering, our ignorance and desires and attachments, in short, our blind passions, are pointed out by the truth of our gathering it to ourselves. "The world is bad, other people are bad, and so even though I have done nothing wrong, still I suffer"—when we think of our lives in this way, it does not shed any light on our suffering. We must question our ignorance, our desires, and how our attachments help increase our suffering.

The truth of suffering and the truth of gathering it to to ourselves point to the truth about ourselves and our world of suffering, and its basic cause.

Third, when blind passions die down, and our suffering is greatly lessened, a state of composure prevails. This is the realm of the dying out of suffering itself, "the extinction of suffering." This is a noteworthy truth called the truth of its extinction. Thus, a truly noteworthy ideal is not to have our dreams come true, it is not to win the race, nor is it to have everything that our heart desires. It is an ideal realm where suffering is made extinct.

Finally, there is a path, leading to the extinction of suffering. This is the truth of the Eightfold Path. The truth of the extinction of suffering and the truth of the path are ideals worthy of our attention. It clearly explains a way of practical living that allows us to reach that goal.

It is not simply a matter of thinking: suffering > gathering > extinction > path. It might be easier to understand this as two sets of comparisons: the reality of the truth of suffering versus the ideal of the extinction of suffering, and the cause of the problem in the truth of our gathering it to ourselves versus the means of resolving it in the Truth of the path.

The truth of the Eightfold Path of practical living is made up of the following eight elements: (1) right view, to see things properly, (2) right thought, to think properly, (3) right speech, to use language properly, (4) right action, to conduct oneself properly, (5) right living, to have proper livelihood, (6) right effort, to make proper progress, (7) right mindfulness, to be properly thoughtful of others, (8) right meditation, to properly focus.

When we explain the matter this way, someone will ask who will decide what is proper or not? The answer is, there is no one who decides. We should think of these eight as prefaced by the word "wholesome" in the light of the principle of the Four Noble Truths. Arbitrarily deciding by ourselves what is proper or believing what someone tells us is proper is typical of the ordinary person. We must be careful of this and turn our focus to the compassion of Buddha's Sincerity (True and Real).

## What is Buddhism's Bottom Line?

Our textbook explanation has grown rather long, but Buddhism begins from the time we first turn our attention to the Four Noble Truths. Thus, in the truth of suffering explained first, unless we perceive the real world and see that all is suffering, our life as a Buddhist does not begin.

Many Japanese people regard themselves as Buddhists, but when asked what Buddhism is, most of them are unable to answer. All is suffering, that is, in the Buddhist understanding of the world, the Buddhists assume that all living things suffer.

When we gain insight into suffering as informing our existence, and that this is truly what a human being is, our blind passions are clarified as the cause of our suffering. With this in mind, as we seek for the extinction of suffering as the ideal we ought to pursue, we are reoriented and moving toward the ideal. At this time, as light is shed upon this true reality of ours, we are obliged to ask where exactly are we moving toward? This is a matter about which Buddhism makes us sit up and take notice.

We could skip over this, and only understand the matter formally, saying that if our family religion is Jodo Shinshu, then an image of Amida Buddha is the object of reverence in the family altar. When you do that, however, nothing is clarified as to the nature of your existence, and when that fails to happen, your suffering does not become a personal matter of reflection for you.

## Never Giving Up On Someone

Shinran Shonin composed this wasan:

*Seeing the sentient beings of the nembutsu*
*Throughout the worlds, countless as particles, in the ten quarters,*
*The Buddha grasps and never abandons them,*
*And therefore is named "Amida."*

*—Jodo wasan 82*

In this *wasan*, Shinran Shonin used the phrase "to grasp and never abandon" which means that once you have been taken up, you are never discarded. It is like a great heart that would take us under its care, and once having saved us, will never throw us away. Shinran Shonin says that for fulfilling the promise "to grasp and never abandon," Buddha was called Amida, that is, he was praised as Amida Buddha, a symbol of Buddha's Sincerity (True and Real).

What then does "throughout the worlds, countless as particles, in the ten quarters," refer to? This means that Amida Buddha's target of liberation is all of these countless sentient beings. In other words, when we think of the existence of all sentient beings, this means we are thinking of the totality of the interconnectedness of life in its every form. We too exist in that world. Amida Buddha (True and Real) takes as the target of liberation all sentient beings. Amida Buddha's cannot stand not to save us, and will look after us. This is what the *wasan* is saying.

When Amida Buddha turns attention to all the sentient beings and all the countless worlds in the ten quarters and when Amida Buddha turns attention to this one individual that I am, this is a single event, thus the eye with which I see myself deepens, does it not?

## Chapter 6

# Returning to the Foolish Nature of Our Self

*In this body lacking even the tiniest shred*
*of compassion for others.*

— *Shozomatsu wasan* 9

## A Teaching For Us Living Today

Up to now we have touched on the difficulty of expounding on Buddhism in the modern world. In the course of our talk we have had a good look at the problems that come with living in modern society, as well as issues we face individually.

Since this is an age in which Buddhism has had difficulty making headway, it is a good a time as any for us Buddhists to present Buddhism as the teaching that is in accordance with the needs of the time and people. The time means now and the people include myself. Buddhism is suited for me to live with here and now.

Buddhism teaches that things in life do not always turn out the way we wish, and that suffering results when we try to force things to turn out the way we want. Life is suffering is a basic Buddhist teaching and the way to deal with it was explained in an earlier chapter concerning the Four Noble Truths.

I would like to say that the Four Noble Truths, a basic tenet of Buddhism, is not just a theory but it is an easy-to-understand explanation of how to deal with the problem of suffering. At the same time, even knowledge of this truth still might not strike a responsive chord with people in modern life.

Of course there is no need to tell people who are suffering that "Life is suffering" they already know it all too well. However, when people truly hear what Buddhism has to say, that there is a basic cause or reason for our suffering, they will naturally begin to confront the bonno or blind passions that characterize the human condition. And when they notice these afflictions burning within themselves, it will give them insight as to why they suffer as they do when things in life do not always turn out the way they had hoped.

In the age of Sakyamuni Buddha, society was receptive to religious seekers. These seekers would leave their home life behind to undergo ascetic practices, and live by strict regulations. Through this way of life they would hope to reduce their afflictions and in the end become free of them. Even now this way of life is an option, but this does not mean that such a path of religious asceticism is open to all.

What then is one to do in this secular life we are living?

The basic formula of Mahayana Buddhism that was transmitted to China and Japan was that the cause of suffering in life was due to our ignorance of our desires and afflictions. In other words, what we are in need of is true wisdom, and through Buddhist practice it becomes the new norm.

At the core of the Pure Land teaching, it is not necessary for one to leave home life behind and pursue ascetic practices in order to be liberated from blind passion. Instead, it is because I am an unenlightened being mired in afflictions that I am the object of liberation. It is precisely because I am an ordinary fellow with no true wisdom to speak of that the Pure Land path was made available for me.

By the time Shinran Shonin appeared on the scene, the thinking in Pure Land teaching was that, since it was impossible to awaken, or become enlightened, in this world, it would be better for us to journey to a place with more amenable circumstances, that is, a Pure Land where we would undergo religious practice and attain enlightenment. Or it was thought that life in this world was altogether too short, and that it was necessary for us to be born again to continue our religious practice.

## What is Meant By Attaining Birth in the Pure Land?

Shinran Shonin, however, was not inclined to this slow roundabout route, and instead struck upon a sure way to resolve the problem once and for all.

There are many religions that claim their founder was the one who conceived their teachings from scratch, but I think this is incorrect. In the case of Buddhism, Sakyamuni Buddha and other founders of the teachings only took notice of its Truth and were not the ones who created it.

In the case of Shinran Shonin as well, he was the one who first discovered a path resolving the problem which he derived from the teachings of those who had gone before him.

What he discovered was that to be born in the Pure Land of Amida Buddha was to awaken, or receive enlightenment. Nowhere does Shinran Shonin use the phrase, "Embarking on the passage to birth is, as once, the attainment of buddhahood" (*ojo soku jobutsu*). However, in *Ichinen ta'nen mon'i*, he does add a note to the term "the ranks of those sure to attain the Truth" (*shojoju*) to the effect that, one is determined to attain birth, that one's self is sure to attain buddhahood. That is, once the forces that sustain our existence have run their course, we are sure to attain buddhahood.

In its literal meaning the phrase "embarking on the passage to attain birth" means "to go to be born" (*ojo*) in the Pure Land.

This "going" is of a different dimension than what we ordinarily mean by the term. That is, it does not take place on the same plane as when we speak of crossing to the other side of a river; the realm of enlightenment is not there, but exists elsewhere, on a different plane. In this notion of "going to be born," even the person who is born is different from a person being born in this world.

In Buddhism, the goal is to go beyond transmigration. The goal is to achieve a realm where we no longer keep repeating our state of lost wandering, of engaging in one meaningless war after another where people keep killing one another in endless cycle. And so at least we can say that the attainment of buddhahood in the Pure Land is not an extension of the realm of transmigration of our previous life. In the notion of "going to be born" we could say that the world of delusion is transformed into a world of a different dimension.

To say it is of a different dimension means it is useless to think of it in terms of our so-called three-dimensional world. Whatever dimension we try to compare it to gets us nowhere; it is futile, like thinking we are born in the Pure Land with our present bodies intact. In spatial terms it is not a linear extension of our world, nor is it an extension of our temporal senses. That type of understanding falls short. On the other hand, the Pure Land as the expression of Amida Buddha's heart is constantly in rapport with us.

It is the wish of Amida Buddha that this empty false self of mine (a transient thing) be transformed into something other than it is—is this not a good way to think of the notion of embarking on the passage to "birth"? It is a world view that cannot be captured in terms of time and space.

## Is it Possible to Become a Buddha In This Life?

When the forces sustaining our life in this world have run their course, we attain birth in the Pure Land, where this self is assured to attain enlightenment. In Jodo Shinshu this is referred to as the ranks of the truly settled to awaken enlightenment in the present life (*gensho shojoju*).

Before the discovery of the path of birth in the Pure Land, there were three general groups of people: the group of people who would attain buddhahood through practices in this life, the group whose practices would fail, and the group who would take a mistaken path; these were called *shojoju, fujoju, and jakujoju,* respectively. In order to awaken, or become enlightened, however, in the end they were required to overcome the bonds of their physical existence.

As long as people were restricted by the bonds of their physical existence they were rudely reminded of the fact that buddhahood was impossible for them to attain. Shinran Shonin was a person who thought long and hard about this. As long as I am caught in this physical body I am a being to whom the possibility of buddhahood is virtually nil. The only hope for me is in finding more amenable circumstances to practice and to attain buddhahood. The only hope is to embark on the passage to birth that is at once the attainment of buddhahood.

The biggest difference between the gradual attainment of buddhahood and "the path to the Pure Land that is at once the attainment of buddhahood" is that either one is obliged to wait interminably while counting on his ability to attain buddhahood, or he intentionally runs full force into the brick wall of his impossible situation.

It is difficult to attain buddhahood while living in an ordinary secular world. Someone might point out that long ago it was possible to attain buddhahood by leaving your home life and practicing asceticism. There were more than a few who realized enlightenment through ascetic practice around the time when Sakyamuni Buddha was alive. However, with the passage of time this has become immensely difficult.

In a relatively simple society, it might have been possible for people to change themselves and their lifestyle, and to go out and do good deeds. In an age where the world has become more linked together and society has grown more complex, however, it is no longer a simple matter to pursue a monastic life. The secular world and the monastic world have become systematically intertwined with one another.

In the period when Shinran Shonin was on Mount Hiei, the secularization of monastic life had already proceeded to a considerable degree. Among the wasan that he composed are a number that lament that fact. These days, even if there was a person who was to awaken to satori or attain enlightenment, as long as that person has to live in this world, it would of necessity involve some hurtful actions toward other living beings.

The situation now is that the monastic seeker cannot exist without some form of secular support. Even though the monastic and secular are separate spheres, the former is not free from the latter that supports it. In the Mount Hiei of Shinran Shonin's time, the monastic world was under the influence of the aristocratic society that supported the temple and shrine complex. The degeneration of the aristocracy and the contempt with which they treated subordinates were serious problems for Shinran Shonin who experienced them firsthand.

The secularization on Mount Hiei was so extensive that there was no escaping it. One could change places or circumstances, but it was still impossible to awaken, or become enlightened. The dread sense of *mappo*, in an age of uncertainty, that Shinran Shonin experienced was a theme developed in certain Buddhist sutras. It grew from his awareness that his own existence was hopelessly pervaded by secularization. That thought grew more profound with time.

Earlier we had a chance to discuss the problem of the narrow perspective of people today. We might also add that there are a great number of people who have a broad view of things, yet this is not sufficient for them to realize enlightenment.

There is a Buddhist monk in Southeast Asia who has been making earnest attempts at social reform. Once one becomes a Buddhist, it is hard to sit still in the face of the various problems that beset society. Of course, the actions one takes are the actions of this imperfect world, and there is no way to avoid their coming up short. However imperfect one's actions, though, it is better to act than to do nothing at all. This is the rationale for the actions of engaged Buddhism based on awareness.

Basic to these actions is my assumption that somehow I can see it through, that is, I can make my plans succeed. There is no speculation on my part that I cannot make it; it is not a possibility that I entertain. It is only when my efforts are revealed to be imperfect that I begin to realize this imperfect side of myself and ask, "Can I make it?" When this question touches the heart of Amida Buddha, it is with the understanding of oneself as someone who cannot make it, who cannot succeed on his own.

## Compassion Transcends Love

Modern people have a positive take on the word "love."

However, if the sense of love that people have is ego driven, then it turns out to be self-centered and turns into something that is far from the ideal. Indeed, what we call love has both a positive and a negative side. The negative side is the inability to become free of attachment; this is man's limitation. True compassion goes beyond such two-sided love.

As the extreme case of compassion, we might cite Amida Buddha's compassion that extends itself to save a person having no redeeming qualities, like myself just as I am, an ordinary person burdened with bad karma.

When most people set out to "save" someone, they go first to those who are easiest to save. In the case of Amida Buddha, however, just the opposite is true. Amida Buddha goes to the rescue of those who are the most difficult to save. It is because they are difficult to save that Amida Buddha goes to rescue them, catching them all without letting one slip away. Thus, I referred to this form of compassion as compassion in the extreme.

When a person sets out to do good, they do so thinking that they will become good and strive to bring forth a compassionate heart out of such goodness. In the Jodo Shinshu teaching this is called the compassion in the Path of Sages. The most remarkable example of such compassion today is the Dalai Lama. The Dalai Lama is a most energetic person who will embark on a project even though he knows he might not be completely successful. For us Jodo Shinshu followers, it is important to note this partial success.

In contrast to the Path of Sages' model of compassion, there is the compassion in the Pure Land path.

When a person knows that they are saved by Amida Buddha (True and Real), knowing full well that they are imperfect to begin with and never taking their eye off of that fact, they do what there is within their power to do. In this case, my actions are not a form of compassion, but as I stand within the embrace of Amida Buddha's compassion, I ask myself what it is that I can do.

## SELF-POWER AND OTHER POWER

We call the compassion in the Path of Sages "self-power" compassion and the path of the Pure Land "Other Power" compassion, understanding Other Power does not mean that we do nothing and should merely let our lives be consumed by inaction. At the root of our awareness of ourselves as imperfect existences, we must do whatever is possible. Without such self-reflection, we would be wide of the mark to merely depend on Other Power.

Compassion in the Path of Sages model of compassion, "One sympathizes with the plight of other beings, feels for them, and seeks to cradle them" (*Tannisho* 4), just as a mother takes care of her children, feeding them, holding them when they are hurt, nursing them through illness. While there are cases where such compassion succeeds, there are also cases when it does not.

Compassion in the Pure Land Path means, "All one needs to do is to say the nembutsu, which is the mind of Great Compassion that looks after the welfare of every living being perfectly" (*Tannisho* 4). Since it is a mind of Great Compassion that is thorough, this involves the very reason for the Great Compassion to exist. All that one needs do is to say the nembutsu to be liberated by the Compassion of Amida Buddha (True and Real).

"There is a difference between the compassion of the Path of Sages and the compassion of the Pure Land path" (*Tannisho* 4). This difference does not mean that one must choose between one or the other; both are forms of compassion. The difference lies in where they lead.

## Nurturing Self-Awareness

"Awareness is nurtured" is a traditional saying in Jodo Shinshu. When you realize that the heart of compassion you have is imperfect, that awareness of yourself deepens over time. Nurturing this insight is what takes time.

Just when is it exactly that the Buddha Dharma penetrates to the core of your being? It doesn't happen simply because you have a teacher who is a spiritual guide from whom you learn about Buddhism. It is from your experience of that person who was your guide that you realize later on what that person wanted to teach you. One day it all falls into place and you say, "Ah, so that was what my teacher was getting at!" Your guide knew that one day you would figure it out, and he or she left that insight for you to arrive at on your own. This means that your awareness of yourself is being nurtured.

Compassion and sympathy are not the same. For instance, we customarily visit someone who is hospitalized, but doing so might actually be hurtful to the patient. We go there with the intention of encouraging them or cheering them up, but it may actually be a great bother to the patient who has to suffer through these visits.

In an act occasioned by sympathy there still remains a strong element of self-centeredness. There is a wasan composed by Shinran Shonin that said:

*Being without even the slightest love or compassion,*
*How could I hope to benefit sentient beings?*
*If it were not for the ship of the Tathagata's vow,*
*How can the ocean of suffering be crossed?*

*—Shozomatsu wasan, Verses of Lamentation*

It is impossible for a person who does not have even the tiniest bit of compassion for others to think of saving others. Without the working of Amida Buddha, how would it be possible for us to cross the sea of suffering where we have long been caught? — this is what the verse is saying. It is important for us to have a good grasp of what this verse is saying: that we are the persons without the tiniest shred of compassion for others.

We are bodies without the tiniest shred of compassion for others' does not mean, however, that we should not try to do anything for others. Shinran Shonin often employs paradoxical statements, and it would be a mistake to take this statement at face value. He is leveling a critical eye at us and asking us whether we would call our own actions "even in the least compassionate" or "beneficial to others."

Indeed, it is difficult to walk in someone else's shoes. The more filled with good intentions we are, the more difficult this becomes. When we are insensitive to the suffering of others, this leads to our being hurtful toward them. Here, our good intentions are our number one stumbling block. When a person thinks, I am good, I am a good person, this is self-deceit.

One either believes in one's good intentions, or one doubts them. Where do we draw the line? Believing in your own goodness is a danger. On the one hand, without those good intentions it is unlikely that we would choose to act. Indeed, this problem could even be said to involve the so-called turning point from the Path of Sages to the Pure Land path. People assume they are good, otherwise they would refuse to act. On the other hand, as long as you put yourself on the "good person" side of the ledger, you are blind to Buddha's Sincerity (True and Real). You as an imperfect, foolish person never comes into focus.

## Shinran Shonin and Me

Finally, I would like to think about why we are attracted to Shinran Shonin.

I think you will agree that one big attraction is that Shinran Shonin did not represent the rugged, gung-ho seeker. He said not to make a show of being wise, good and dedicated. He accepted life for what it was and people for what they were, and accepted himself in the same vein.

His teacher, Honen Shonin, also had this "as-it-is" attitude, where he was receptive to the wise as the wise and the foolish as the foolish. Shinran Shonin adopted this attitude from him and taught that there is a way for the foolish person to be liberated as he or she is. He taught that those who were inwardly false and insincere should not pretend to be wise and good. Being near Honen Shonin, Shinran Shonin must have learned a lesson in just how to accept himself as he was. No doubt Honen Shonin served as a life-sized mirror in which Shinran Shonin saw his own existence reflected. In this way he constantly made inquiry into himself.

Shinran Shonin accepted human nature for what it was. He did not play up its good side or play down the parts that were inconvenient. He readily admitted his foolish nature. He was the first to stand up and admit he was an ordinary foolish person. Perhaps that is the reason why people down through the ages have been willing to listen to the teaching of Shinran Shonin.

Shinran Shonin did not place himself on a higher level when he said that he would accept me, but instead taught that I am where he was accepted; he showed that this is an instance of the working of Amida Buddha's (True and Real) compassion. This points to a path wherein we can live again, even for modern people who have been swept along by the nihilism of the modern age steeped in its human-centered way of thinking.

At the same time this places a heavy demand on us. The demand is that we shift our focus from our human-centered way of thinking to that where we make a clear discernment between what is real and what is not. In a sense, it demands that we accept the discernment that "only the nembutsu is real."

Is not the nihilism of the present age derived from the same inability to awaken to what is true and real that Shinran Shonin had encountered? Modern society, based on scientific thinking and the spirit of positivism, has declared Truth as unnecessary and has eliminated it from consideration. Physical laws and marketing principles, as well as political science and technology, have become the principles around which our world turns. It is easier to dispense with the teachings that Shinran Shonin encountered and to live a life devoid of deep thought and introspection. When living a self-centered life is primary, however, we may well live a convenient life, but lack a sense of meaning. Even we have become nothing more than another commodity. That is where nihilism is taking us.

Unless we become aware of our own foolishness, our innate feeling or knowledge of being a part of and connected to "all sentient beings" will never gain the prominence in our lives it deserves. The more human-centered and self-centered our society becomes, the more I, as a human being, am being stripped of my very humanity.

We stand at a major turning point in history. First, it is imperative that we gain a direct insight into ourselves. As just one being among many living beings, we must become aware of our blind passions or afflictions. We must turn to Amida Buddha (True and Real) to be accepted as we are, however imperfect and foolish we may be.

# Bibliography

Ariyoshi, Sawako 有吉佐和子 (1913–1984), *Fukugo osen* 複合汚染 [Compound contamination], 2 vols., Tokyo: Shincho-sha, 1974, 1975.

Asai, Narumi 浅井成海, b. 1935, *Shinshu o manabu: Gu ni kaerite* 真宗を学ぶ: 愚にかえりて [What We Can Learn from Shinshu], Kyoto: Nagata Bunshodo, 1996.

Carson, Rachel (1907–1964), *Silent Spring*, Greenwich, CT: Fawcett, 1962.

Ishida, Keiwa, b. 1928, 'Gendai ni okeru Shinshu kenkyu no kadai: Takeuchi Yoshinori Sensei no Go-gyoseki wo megutte' 現代における真宗研究の課題: 武内義ノリ先生の御業績をめぐって [Recent topics in Shinshu research: Regarding the writings of Professor Yoshinori Takeuchi], *Shinshu kenkyu* 47:227-242, 2003. See p 230.

Kato, Shuichi (1919–2008), *Shinran: jusan seiki no ichimen* 親鸞: 一三世紀思想の一面 [Shinran: One aspect of the thought systems in the thirteenth century], Tokyo: Shincho-sha, 1960.

Kayama, Rika, author of numerous works. One with an English title is, *I Miss Me*, Tokyo: Seishun Shuppan-sha, 2000.

Meadows, Donella, H. (1941–2001), et al., *The Limits to Growth*: A report for the Club of Rome's project on the predicament of mankind, London: Earth Island, 1972.

Ohtani, Koshin 大谷光真 (b. 1945), *Gu no chikara* 愚の力: Tokyo: Bungei Shunju, 2009.

Rennyo Shonin, *Gobunsho*. For a recent English translation, see G. M. Nagao, ed., Shin Buddhism Translation Series, *Letters of Rennyo*, Kyoto: Hongwanji International Center, 2000.

*Sanbutsu ge*, or 'Verses in Praise of the Buddha', a section of *The Larger Sutra of Immeasurable Life*. For a recent modern English translation, see *The Three Pure Land Sutras*, Volume II: *The Sutra on the Buddha of Immeasurable Life*, The Shin Buddhism Translation Series Translation Committee, trans.; H. Inagaki, ed., Kyoto: Jodo Shinshu Hongwanji-ha, 2009.

Shinran Shonin (1173-1263) *The Collected Works of Shinran,* Volume 1. Gadjin M. Nagao, ed., Kyoto: Jodo Shinshu Honganji-ha, 1997.

— *Shozomatsu wasan*: Shinran's Hymns on the Last Age, trans. Ryukoku University Translation Center, Kyoto: Ryukoku University Translation Center, 1980.

Suzuki, Masao 鈴木理生, b. 1926, *Edo no machi wa hone darake* 江戸の町は骨だらけ [The town of Edo is littered with bones], Tokyo: Ohtoh Shoboh, 2002.

Uchida, Tatsuru 内田樹, *b.* 1950, *Karyu shiko: manabanai kodomo-tachi, hatarakanai wakamono-tachi* 下流志向:学ばない子どもたち働かない若者たち [The downward trend: Children who do not learn, young people who do not work] Tokyo: Kodansha, 2009.

Yamazaki, Ryumyo, *b.* 1943, 'Why Shinran now? Returning to the simple side of our self, with a spring in our step' (December 18, 2007, *Tokyo Shinbun*, evening edition).

Yuien, 1222–1289, comp., *Tannisho*, ca. 1289. For a recent revised edition see, *A Record in Lament of Divergences: A Translation of the Tannisho*, trans. and ed. English Translation Committee, H. Inagaki, gen. ed., Shin Buddhism Translation Series, Jodo Shinshu Studies and Research Center, Kyoto: Hongwanji Shuppansha, 1995, rev. ed. 2003.

# ACKNOWLEDGMENT

Once again, I am deeply grateful to Monshu Koshin Ohtani and the Nishi Hongwanji International Department for granting us permission to publish the English translation of *Gu no chikara*. Even though the Japanese title literally translated as "Our foolish being" does not correspond to the English title "The Buddha's Call to Awaken" the message that Monshu Ohtani delivers, in essence, is to awaken from our foolish ways.

I am sincerely thankful to Reverend Michio Tokunaga, Kangaku, (Hongwanji scholar) Jodo Shinshu Hongwanji-ha, International Department in Kyoto, Japan for asking the American Buddhist Study Center (ABSC) to edit, design, publish, and distribute "The Buddha's Call to Awaken." On behalf of the ABSC board of directors we were grateful and delighted to be given this opportunity to publish, thereby helping to spread the teachings of Shin Buddhism.

Thank you, Rev. Wayne Yokoyama for your accurate translation of *Gu no chikara* and helping us as well in the final edit. This was a difficult book to translate because Monshu introduced many difficult concepts that Rev. Yokoyama had to translate into English and retain the same connotation.

Editing this book was done in two stages. First, Rev. Tatsuo Muneto, Director of the Buddhist Study Center at the Honpa Mission of Hawaii in Honolulu carefully compared the original Japanese text against the English translation. Rev. Muneto consulted with Rev. Tokunaga on many chapters in this book for clarification. I am so grateful to Rev. Muneto for his uncompromising stance and

Rev. Tokunaga for his expert knowledge to enhance Rev. Yokoyama's translation. Thank you.

The final editing was handled by Rev. Marvin Harada's team at the Orange Country Buddhist Church. My deep appreciation to Kay and Jim Mitchell, Jon Turner, Amy Iwamasa and Bill Dearth for all the hours they put into this project. Like Rev. Muneto, the Buddhist Education Center group were so dedicated and devoted to cleaning up the translation to make it an easy to read and understandable book even to beginners.

Thank you, Dr. Alfred Bloom for your help us in clarifying some of the passages in this book and writing an absolutely definitive and wonderful Introduction.

Lastly, I want to give a very special thank you to Arlene Kato for designing a beautiful front cover and to Scott Mitchell for granting us permission to use his professionally taken photograph of Amida Buddha, from our Jodo Shinshu Center, as our cover artwork. Arlene also formatted this book and worked hard to make sure all the changes were accurate. She is an entire art and production department and is a very dedicated designer. Thank you, Arlene.

In closing with palms together, I humbly thank Monshu Koshin Ohtani for writing this book and teaching us how foolishly destructive mankind can be.

In Gassho,
Hoshin Seki
President
American Buddhist Study Center